Joyce Appleby on *Thomas Jefferson*
Louis Auchincloss on *Theodore Roosevelt*
Jean H. Baker on *James Buchanan*
H. W. Brands on *Woodrow Wilson*
Douglas Brinkley on *Gerald R. Ford*
Josiah Bunting III on *Ulysses S. Grant*
James MacGregor Burns and Susan Dunn on *George Washington*
Charles W. Calhoun on *Benjamin Harrison*
Gail Collins on *William Henry Harrison*
Robert Dallek on *Harry S. Truman*
John W. Dean on *Warren G. Harding*
John Patrick Diggins on *John Adams*
E. L. Doctorow on *Abraham Lincoln*
Elizabeth Drew on *Richard M. Nixon*
Annette Gordon-Reed on *Andrew Johnson*
Henry F. Graff on *Grover Cleveland*
David Greenberg on *Calvin Coolidge*
Gary Hart on *James Monroe*
Hendrik Hertzberg on *Jimmy Carter*
Roy Jenkins on *Franklin Delano Roosevelt*
Zachary Karabell on *Chester Alan Arthur*
Lewis H. Lapham on *William Howard Taft*
William E. Leuchtenburg on *Herbert Hoover*
Timothy Naftali on *George Bush*
Kevin Phillips on *William McKinley*
Robert V. Remini on *John Quincy Adams*
Ira M. Rutkow on *James A. Garfield*
John Seigenthaler on *James K. Polk*
Hans L. Trefousse on *Rutherford B. Hayes*
Tom Wicker on *Dwight D. Eisenhower*
Ted Widmer on *Martin Van Buren*
Sean Wilentz on *Andrew Jackson*
Garry Wills on *James Madison*

# Andrew Jackson

Sean Wilentz

# Andrew Jackson

**THE AMERICAN PRESIDENTS**

ARTHUR M. SCHLESINGER, JR., GENERAL EDITOR

Times Books

HENRY HOLT AND COMPANY, NEW YORK

Times Books
Henry Holt and Company, LLC
*Publishers since 1866*
175 Fifth Avenue
New York, New York 10010
www.henryholt.com

Frontispiece: Collection of the New-York Historical Society,
accession number 1858.11

Library of Congress Cataloging-in-Publication Data

Wilentz, Sean.
 Andrew Jackson / Sean Wilentz—1st ed.
  p. cm.—(The American presidents series)
 Includes bibliographical references and index.
 ISBN-13: 978-0-8050-6925-9
 ISBN-10: 0-8050-6925-9
 1. Jackson, Andrew, 1767–1845. 2. Presidents—United States—
Biography. 3. United States—Politics and government—1829–1837.
I. Title.  II. American presidents series (Times Books (Firm))

E382.W74 2005
973.5'6'092—dc22
[B]                                                    2005052857

First Edition 2005

Printed in the United States of America
1  3  5  7  9  10  8  6  4  2

*To S.B.*

Bear me out in it, thou great democratic God! who didst not refuse to the swart convict, Bunyan, the pale, poetic pearl; Thou who didst clothe with doubly hammered leaves of finest gold, the stumped and paupered arm of old Cervantes; Thou who didst pick up Andrew Jackson from the pebbles; who didst hurl him upon a war-horse; who didst thunder him higher than a throne! Thou who, in all Thy mighty, earthly marchings, ever cullest Thy selectest champions from the kingly commons; bear me out in it, O God!

—HERMAN MELVILLE,
*Moby-Dick; or, The Whale*
1851

# Contents

# Editor's Note

The president is the central player in the American political order. That would seem to contradict the intentions of the Founding Fathers. Remembering the horrid example of the British monarchy, they invented a separation of powers in order, as Justice Brandeis later put it, "to preclude the exercise of arbitrary power." Accordingly, they divided the government into three allegedly equal and coordinate branches—the executive, the legislative, and the judiciary.

But a system based on the tripartite separation of powers has an inherent tendency toward inertia and stalemate. One of the three branches must take the initiative if the system is to move. The executive branch alone is structurally capable of taking that initiative. The Founders must have sensed this when they accepted Alexander Hamilton's proposition in the Seventieth Federalist that "energy in the executive is a leading character in the definition of good government." They thus envisaged a strong president—but within an equally strong system of constitutional accountability. (The term *imperial presidency* arose in the 1970s to describe the situation when the balance between power and accountability is upset in favor of the executive.)

The American system of self-government thus comes to focus in the presidency—"the vital place of action in the system," as Woodrow Wilson put it. Henry Adams, himself the great-grandson and grandson of presidents as well as the most brilliant of American historians, said that the American president "resembles the commander of a ship at sea. He must have a helm to grasp, a course to steer, a port to seek." The men in the White House (thus far only men, alas) in steering their chosen courses have shaped our destiny as a nation.

Biography offers an easy education in American history, rendering the past more human, more vivid, more intimate, more accessible, more connected to ourselves. Biography reminds us that presidents are not supermen. They are human beings too, worrying about decisions, attending to wives and children, juggling balls in the air, and putting on their pants one leg at a time. Indeed, as Emerson contended, "There is properly no history; only biography."

Presidents serve us as inspirations, and they also serve us as warnings. They provide bad examples as well as good. The nation, the Supreme Court has said, has "no right to expect that it will always have wise and humane rulers, sincerely attached to the principles of the Constitution. Wicked men, ambitious of power, with hatred of liberty and contempt of law, may fill the place once occupied by Washington and Lincoln."

The men in the White House express the ideals and the values, the frailties and the flaws, of the voters who send them there. It is altogether natural that we should want to know more about the virtues and the vices of the fellows we have elected to govern us. As we know more about them, we will know more about ourselves. The French political philosopher Joseph de Maistre said, "Every nation has the government it deserves."

At the start of the twenty-first century, forty-two men have made it to the Oval Office. (George W. Bush is counted our forty-third president, because Grover Cleveland, who served nonconsecutive terms, is counted twice.) Of the parade of presidents, a dozen or so lead the polls periodically conducted by historians and political scientists. What makes a great president?

Great presidents possess, or are possessed by, a vision of an ideal

America. Their passion, as they grasp the helm, is to set the ship of state on the right course toward the port they seek. Great presidents also have a deep psychic connection with the needs, anxieties, dreams of people. "I do not believe," said Wilson, "that any man can lead who does not act . . . under the impulse of a profound sympathy with those whom he leads—a sympathy which is insight—an insight which is of the heart rather than of the intellect."

"All of our great presidents," said Franklin D. Roosevelt, "were leaders of thought at a time when certain ideas in the life of the nation had to be clarified." So Washington incarnated the idea of federal union, Jefferson and Jackson the idea of democracy, Lincoln union and freedom, Cleveland rugged honesty. Theodore Roosevelt and Wilson, said FDR, were both "moral leaders, each in his own way and his own time, who used the presidency as a pulpit."

To succeed, presidents not only must have a port to seek but they must convince Congress and the electorate that it is a port worth seeking. Politics in a democracy is ultimately an educational process, an adventure in persuasion and consent. Every president stands in Theodore Roosevelt's bully pulpit.

The greatest presidents in the scholars' rankings, Washington, Lincoln, and Franklin Roosevelt, were leaders who confronted and overcame the republic's greatest crises. Crisis widens presidential opportunities for bold and imaginative action. But it does not guarantee presidential greatness. The crisis of secession did not spur Buchanan or the crisis of depression spur Hoover to creative leadership. Their inadequacies in the face of crisis allowed Lincoln and the second Roosevelt to show the difference individuals make to history. Still, even in the absence of first-order crisis, forceful and persuasive presidents—Jefferson, Jackson, James K. Polk, Theodore Roosevelt, Ronald Reagan—are able to impose their own priorities on the country.

The diverse drama of the presidency offers a fascinating set of tales. Biographies of American presidents constitute a chronicle of wisdom and folly, nobility and pettiness, courage and cunning, forthrightness and deceit, quarrel and consensus. The turmoil perennially swirling around the White House illuminates the heart of the American democracy.

It is the aim of the American Presidents series to present the grand panorama of our chief executives in volumes compact enough for the busy reader, lucid enough for the student, authoritative enough for the scholar. Each volume offers a distillation of character and career. I hope that these lives will give readers some understanding of the pitfalls and potentialities of the presidency and also of the responsibilities of citizenship. Truman's famous sign—"The buck stops here"—tells only half the story. Citizens cannot escape the ultimate responsibility. It is in the voting booth, not on the presidential desk, that the buck finally stops.

—Arthur M. Schlesinger, Jr.

# Andrew Jackson

# Prologue

## Jackson and the Age of the Democratic Revolution

In the early spring of 1835, the renowned engraver and painter Asher Durand executed the finest portrait of Andrew Jackson made during Jackson's presidency. The artist could extract only four or five sittings from his irascible, distracted subject. Jackson, Durand reported, "has been part of the time in a pretty good humor, but some times he gets his 'dander up' & smokes his pipe prodigiously." Still, the final picture was candid and persuasive, showing a care-worn, elegantly attired old man, his cheeks and forehead deeply lined, lips clenched over toothless gums, and black-coffee eyes emanating both melancholy and determination.* One New York critic pronounced it "not merely a likeness but a facsimile."[1]

Strong as it was, the rendering was incomplete—for hidden beneath Jackson's shock of stiff white hair was a deep and nasty scar. As a boy soldier during the American Revolution, Jackson had been captured by British dragoons and ordered to scrape the mud off an officer's boots. When Jackson claimed the status of a prisoner of war and refused to be shamed, the officer slashed him with a sword, nearly severing several fingers and cutting a permanent trench into the boy's skull. Although it would not be the last violent badge of courage and honor Jackson would receive, it would remain his greatest source of pride, an eternal reminder of his patriotic suffering and dedication.

*Durand's portrait is reproduced as the frontispiece of this volume.

A year before Jackson sat for Durand's portrait, while the Senate was debating whether to censure him for presidential misconduct, he learned that a Whig congressman planned to introduce articles of impeachment—and to charge that the stories about the wartime slashing had been invented as a campaign ploy.

"The damned infernal scoundrel!" Jackson snarled to his close friend and adviser Francis Blair. "Put your finger here, Mr. Blair." The president parted his hair, and Blair was shocked to discover that he could fit his entire finger inside the scarred gash.[2]

Fearless, principled, and damaged, Andrew Jackson was one of the fiercest and most controversial men ever to serve as president of the United States. Like few other presidents until the present era— Jefferson, Lincoln, FDR—Jackson inspired love and hatred, with no apparent middle ground. "Talk of him as the second Washington!" the New York patrician Philip Hone wrote with sarcasm and disgust in 1833. "It won't do now: Washington was only the first Jackson." Hone and his conservative friends in truth thought of Jackson as an American Caesar, who had stirred up the blockhead masses, seized power, and installed a new despotism. Jackson's more radical critics likewise detested him as a dangerous demagogue. But to his admirers, Jackson was the most courageous man in the country, the one leader, a North Carolinian observed, who "could have withstood the overwhelming influence" of the nation's "corrupt Aristocracy," to safeguard equal rights and American democracy.[3]

There are plenty of signals in our culture today that we are *supposed* to admire Jackson as a great American. His picture is on the twenty-dollar bill. His plantation home outside Nashville, the Hermitage, is a national historic monument. The imposing statue of Jackson in his general's uniform, rearing on horseback, still dominates Lafayette Square Park as it has for more than a century and a half, with Jackson doffing his half-moon officer's cap at the White House. Separate polls of historians who vary widely in their assessments of the presidents consistently rate Jackson near the top, just below Washington, Lincoln, and FDR. Yet apart from Jefferson, no past president has suffered harsher criticism from recent historians than has Jackson—no longer a hero, in many circles, but an ignorant, violent slaveholder who suppressed the abolitionists, ruined the American economy, and perpetrated genocide on the Indians. The attacks rival in their intensity those loosed on Jackson from both the Right and the Left in his own time.

Modern scholarship was initially shaped—as in many ways it continues to be—by Arthur M. Schlesinger, Jr.'s, admiring *Age of Jackson*, published in 1945. Rejecting earlier portrayals of Old Hickory as a western outsider battling eastern privilege, Schlesinger narrated the politics of the 1820s and 1830s as more of a struggle between classes than between regions, focused on Jackson's famous war against the Second Bank of the United States. Urban workingmen and distressed small farmers, Schlesinger argued, united behind the noble liberal Jackson, a true common-born man of the people, in an all-out struggle against shortsighted bankers and businessmen. Over the succeeding decades, numerous biographers and historians, including Robert V. Remini and Charles Sellers, offered modified versions of Schlesinger's interpretation. Most recently, these admirers have depicted Jackson as the enemy of a soulless "market revolution" that transformed American economic and social life and widened material inequality.

Other historians over the past thirty years, however, have presented intensely negative assessments of both Jackson and his presidency. Some have drawn on the critical ripostes to Schlesinger that appeared in the 1940s and 1950s, notably by Richard Hofstadter and Bray Hammond. Far from being a forerunner of democratic liberalism, Hofstadter and Hammond claimed, Jackson represented an aggressive, self-promoting class of entrepreneurs who pioneered the cutthroat, laissez-faire capitalism that would come to dominate the country during the Gilded Age. Later scholars, led by Michael Paul Rogin, focused on the even darker sides of Jackson's presidency—his unwavering dedication to Indian removal and his attacks on abolitionism—and recast Jackson as an avatar of racism. Rogin's Freudian interpretation of what he described as Jackson's genocidal viciousness against the Indians also signaled a new emphasis on Jackson's psychology and character as the taproots of his politics. In later variations, Jackson has appeared as a traumatized product of the raucous southern backcountry, whose unbalanced quest for manly honor—what one scholar has called his "search for vindication"—caused him to lash out at chimerical threats ranging from the Cherokees to the Second Bank. If, as the 1960s slogan ran, the personal is the political, then Jackson was a leader twisted by inner rages—a man, one historian has recently written, whose arrogance should repel all "who identify with the world's oppressed and seek remedies for the sins of violence and covetousness."[4]

This clash of historical interpretations of Jackson is confusing. Behind it lie long-term changes in basic political ideas and sensibilities that make assessing Jackson's legacy—or that of any political figure before the Civil War era—extremely difficult. The basic American vocabulary is very different now than it was in the 1830s. Should Jackson, for example, be considered a liberal or a conservative? Today, liberalism is loosely equated, sometimes in caricatured ways, with an interventionist federal government, a distrust of the free market, a dedication to civil rights (especially for blacks, women, and homosexuals), a wariness of the military, and a weakness for educated, even elitist cultural prejudices. Conservatives, according to the same broad depictions, supposedly believe in state rights, want to reduce government's involvement with the economy, are skeptical about or hostile to civil rights legislation, idolize the military, and emanate a down-home, anti-elitist (some say anti-intellectual) style. By these lights, Jackson, a southwestern slaveholder and military hero with populist appeal, who believed in limited government, ought to be considered a forerunner of Ronald Reagan and George W. Bush—a view some modern conservative commentators are eager to endorse.

Such transposing of political labels in the search for political forerunners is anachronistic, deceptive, and often distorted. The idea, for example, that there has always been a pro–big government party and a laissez-faire party, and that presidents can be judged by which they adhere to, is as useless in interpreting the politics of the 1830s as it is for interpreting our own time. American political parties have always blended "small government" and "big government" policies. Today, the Republican Party rejects federal regulation of business, but shows a robust willingness to regulate the affairs of individuals over certain social, cultural, and political issues. Without embarrassment, Republican leaders look to the federal courts, sometimes at the direct expense of state rights, to secure what they consider a favorable outcome. The Democratic Party, meanwhile, is much more attentive to regulating business, but comparatively laissez-faire on cultural and social matters—and, when it suits them, Democrats kick and scream about violations of state rights. Likewise, in Jackson's day, both the Jackson Democrats and their Whig Party opponents favored minimal government on some issues but not on others. This does not mean that political parties are unprincipled and bend their ideas merely to advance their own interests; it means that party politics cannot be reduced to simplistic formulas about federal versus state powers, in either the past or the present.

There is an additional danger in confusing the means and ends of one historical period for those of another. Before the advent of large national corporations and heavy industry, American liberals commonly pursued their goals with what are now considered conservative policies, and vice versa. Jackson, for example, sought to sever the connection of government and private business, which sounds today like quintessential hands-off conservatism. Yet he did so because he wanted to discourage the rise of a small elite of monied men who enjoyed disproportional political power—one of the overarching aims of American liberalism since the New Deal. In other areas—his attack on state rights nullification and his vaunting of the Union, his disregard for what would now be called "faith-based" politics—Jackson defied much of what have become modern conservative ideas. But in still other areas—especially regarding civil liberties, Indian removal, and racial equality—he looks like a liberal's nightmare.

All efforts to judge Andrew Jackson by political standards other than his own, and those of his time, are doomed from the start. And by the criteria of the 1830s, Jackson was regarded as a champion of equal rights and democracy, in line with the maxim, delivered in his first annual message, that *"the majority is to govern."* There were some exceptions, such as the abolitionist William Lloyd Garrison, who condemned Jackson as a slaveholder and upholder of sinful inequality. The British radical William Cobbett, however, hailed him as "the greatest soldier and greatest statesman, whose name has ever yet appeared upon the records of valour and of wisdom." The Scots-born émigré Frances Wright—a heterodox feminist, freethinker, and antislavery firebrand known as "the Red Harlot of Infidelity"—thought Jackson was "the true saviour of the species." The iconoclastic New York editor William Leggett came to dispute sharply Jackson's stance on slavery, but nevertheless thought him "the leader and champion of the people," who stood "at the head of the Democracy of the world, fighting its battles, and stemming the tide of selfish interest combined with unprincipled ambition." Eminent conservatives saw similar things in Jackson, but with dismay, calling him the foremost advocate of what the learned jurist James Kent denounced as "the democracy of numbers and radicalism."[5]

In the grander scheme of national and world politics, Jackson aligned himself, in his own mind and those of his supporters, with the forces of movement rather than of order, on the side of egalitarianism and against privilege. Therein lies his claim to historical greatness. Jackson's life and public career coincided almost exactly with what historians have called the Age of the Democratic Revolution in the Atlantic world, commencing with the American Revolution and concluding with the failed European revolutions of 1848.[6] It was an age of intense political upheavals, in which the friends of Enlightenment, backed by popular unrest, challenged the unquestioned authority of royalty and aristocracy. It was also a time of deep economic and social change. Enormous commercial and industrial innovations proved liberating for some and oppressive for others. Paternalistic hierarchies of family, clan, and church receded in favor of increasingly unbounded claims to individual rights and self-reliance.

The outcomes of this turmoil varied widely. The French Revolution of 1789 degenerated into tyranny before giving way to royalist restoration. On the rest of the continent, reaction held hard sway over liberalism and antimonarchical revolt through the middle of the nineteenth century. In Britain, the repression of the late eighteenth and early nineteenth centuries prefaced a period of measured political reform that, though it won the abolition of slavery in Britain's overseas colonies, could achieve no more at home than the restrained Reform Bill of 1832, which ended some of the most flagrant inequalities of representation but left intact much of the landed aristocracy's power and privilege. Only in the United States—and there in incomplete and sometimes brutally paradoxical ways—did the Age of the Democratic Revolution break through to create enduring new political realities and possibilities. In a universe of kings and nobles, the American Republic stood alone as what Jefferson called, in 1801, the repository of "the world's best hope"—a government in which the citizenry and not royalty were sovereign.[7]

Andrew Jackson dedicated his presidency to vindicating and expanding that hope by ridding the nation of a recrudescent corrupt privilege that he believed was killing it. His victories as well as his imposing presence have stamped his name on an entire period in American history covering the three decades after the War of 1812, known familiarly as the Jacksonian era. Jackson was not, though, an archetypal or predictable product of his time—what the greatest American philosopher in Jacksonian America (and no great admirer of Jackson's), Ralph Waldo Emerson, called a "representative man." Jackson was deeply paradoxical. Orphaned young, and reliant on his own wits, he was a parvenu who also embraced a paternalist southern code of honor and vengeance more typical of traditional landed classes than of the rambunctious new democratic world. Although his political hero was Thomas Jefferson, the bookish upholder of detached reason, Jackson was preeminently a man of action, unschooled, and (compared to his presidential predecessors) ill-read, touted by his supporters as "nature's nobleman" and prized more for his instincts than for his intellect. (According to one, not wholly reliable, report, Jefferson considered Jackson, as a military man, too dangerous to be president.) Jackson was ranked, by friend and foe alike, as a social outsider, with an unpolished plebeian sensibility unlike any yet seen in an American president—yet he was also a member in good standing of Tennessee's slaveholding planter elite, described by many as gracious, even knightly. Although the head of the first mass democratic party in world history, he often acted on the basis of fierce personal loyalties (and hatreds), and took positions that seemed at odds with his stated principles, sometimes frustrating and sometimes confusing his political managers. Despite his contradictions, Jackson came to be regarded, for better or worse, as the embodiment of the democratic idea. Opposition to Jackson and his party was hopeless, the young anti-Jacksonian William Henry Seward wrote in 1835, so long as the American people supported the principle that Jackson represented: "That principle is Democracy. . . . It is with them, the poor against the rich; and it is not to be disguised."[8]

One of the greatest challenges Jackson poses to any biographer or historian is to make sense of his paradoxes and contradictions without slighting either his defects or his achievements. Another is to describe the irksome personality of this strange democrat without allowing that personality to overwhelm everything else about him, including his ideas and principles—and without ignoring his ability to change. I have no interest in adding to the abundant literature of retrospective psychological interpretations concerning Jackson's presidency. I do not believe that a particular loss or trauma—the "Rosebud" syndrome of Orson Welles's Charles Foster Kane—can adequately explain any political career. Like other, even greater presidents, Jackson, by the time he reached the White House, had advanced well beyond his youthful trials and exploits. Abraham Lincoln at age forty—a hack Whig politician and disappointed officeholder, out to make as much money as he could from his law practice—gave little presentiment of the antislavery war president and the philosophical author of the Gettysburg Address he would become. Likewise, Jackson at forty, a dueling southwestern gentlemen and would-be generalissimo, offered few hints of the democratic leader who would emerge twenty years later.

Still, after reading the sources on Jackson's life and thought, one cannot help being drawn back (as he was) to young Andrew's patriotic ardor and torment during the American Revolution—an experience that proved fundamental to his ideas and his actions for the rest of his life. Being "[b]rought up under the tyranny of Britain" and "losing every thing that was dear to me" in the struggle for independence, he once wrote, made it his sworn duty to uphold republican government "and the independent rights of our nation."[9] Not only did he suffer permanent disfigurement fighting the British; the combat and the disease endemic among American prisoners of war cost him his mother (his father was already long dead) and both of his siblings. The personal cannot explain the political—but in Jackson's case, they reinforced each other mightily. His thinking and his spirit enlarged as he grew older, but basic themes recurred—themes that combined patriotism, manly honor, and, in time, what he came to champion as democracy. Jackson is best understood, I believe, in connection with these themes, as both a product of the American Revolution and a shaper of the larger Age of the Democratic Revolution in which he lived.

From the Revolution on, Jackson's hatred of monarchy, aristocracy, and political privilege—especially of the British variety—formed a screen through which he viewed the world. He always feared that the aristocratic British and their American allies and imitators—defiant Indians, overfed financiers, sectional extremists—threatened to undo the American Revolution and the Constitution of the United States. Unless checked, these forces would either dismember the Union from without or subvert it from within—bending the Constitution and the institutions of government to the will of a minority, substituting corruption and favoritism

for the formally classless Republic designed by the nation's
founders. In Jackson's mind, vindicating his personal honor and
protecting the Revolution's legacy were always entwined, two parts
of the same mission.

From his first fleeting years in Congress as a frontiersman representative in the 1790s through his military exploits in the War of
1812, Jackson believed that he and the nation were embattled by
the forces of rotten despotism. *"Who are we? and for what are we
going to fight,"* Jackson proclaimed in a handwritten call for enlist-
ments early in the War of 1812. "[A]re we the titled Slaves of
George the third? the military conscripts of Napoleon the great? or
the frozen peasants of the Russian Czar? No—we are the freeborn
sons of america; the citizens of the only republick now existing in
the world." Later, when preparing for the Battle of New Orleans, he
wrote to his wife, Rachel, and recalled his boyhood agonies: "I owe
to Britain a debt of retaliatory vengeance; should our forces meet I
trust I shall pay the debt." Robbed of the presidency in 1824 by, he
believed, sinister, oligarchic machinations—another blow to his
honor—he vowed to confound the corrupters by winning the
White House four years later, and then cleansing the federal government of all traces of aristocracy. As president, he assailed anything he construed as either undemocratic heresy or a potential
threat to democracy and the Union, by widening the field of executive appointments through rotation in office, excoriating the South
Carolina nullifiers, destroying the Second Bank of the United
States—and silencing the radical abolitionists. Always he went into
political battle with his continuing personal drama in mind, but
also to defend principles much larger than himself.[10]

It is little wonder that such a vehement, towering figure inspired
both loyalty and loathing—and that he still does. Yet Jackson also
learned, after painful experience, how to temper his vehemence,
and how to deploy it when necessary in service to his evolving
political ideals. And although he sometimes appeared (and strove
to appear) to be larger than life, his times shaped him as much as he
shaped them. Jackson was not responsible for many of the demo-

cratic changes, including the expansion of the suffrage, that still adhere to his legend. He was democracy's beneficiary as well as its emblem. Many of the political ideals he came to embrace—radical "hard money" economics, constitutional nationalism, a strong hand for the executive branch—had barely begun to move him before he was elected to the White House. His capacity to build upon his anti-aristocratic instincts, to learn from his mistakes, and still command the loyalty of others, is what finally defined his presidency. And his success in advancing his principles, above and beyond his volatile personality, is what divided public opinion about him so sharply.

Jackson, one of the oldest men ever elected to the presidency, came of age at the dawn of the Age of the Democratic Revolution, when sober, responsible Americans—including patriots such as George Washington and John Adams—worried that their new Republic might be carrying equality too far, and building too democratic a political system. Some, like Adams, became convinced that men were inherently unequal, certainly in their natural capacities and even in the capacities they acquired in life. Jackson, like Jefferson before him, understood that such objections to democracy and equality were beside the point. They agreed that there was no such thing as universal equality. Some persons were blessed with greater intellect, talent, and good fortune than others, and those vicissitudes of chance and providence could not be altered. But the real issue facing America and the world was not natural inequality—it was artificial inequality, the ways in which some men manufactured privilege for their own benefit. Jackson believed that the American government was designed to undo artificial inequality, and that this idea was the foundation of the American Revolution and the federal Constitution. He ran his presidency accordingly.

Jackson pushed the idea of democratic popular sovereignty farther than any previous American president, but he did not see injustice in many of the inequalities repugnant to later generations of Americans, and even to some Americans in his own time.

Inequalities that others deemed artificial—especially between blacks and whites, Indians and settlers, men and women—appeared to Jackson, as they did to most of his American contemporaries, perfectly natural, the results of an inscrutable dispensation. Compared to some of his own supporters, Jackson's conception of democracy was limited, especially over the issue of slavery. As president, he was, in many respects, a transitional figure in the history of American democratic politics, who stood midway between the founding of the Republic and its rebirth in the Civil War.

Interpreting Jackson as a transitional democrat helps make sense of his presidency, including its manifest failures and moral blind spots, its enormous tragedies as well as its triumphs. It also helps us make sense of the figure rendered by Asher Durand in 1835. Although Durand did not capture everything, he did portray the toll that life had taken on Andrew Jackson, in his rise from abject obscurity, his military battles and personal duels, and his rages against his enemies—and, Jackson believed, the Republic's. The awkward plainness of Jackson's crevassed face belies his fine dress. There is intense pain as well as sadness in his eyes, but also a glinting resolve. It is a portrait of the president as beleaguered democrat, for whom democracy's expansion, as he understood it, was the measure of his own success as well as his country's.

His travails began in the disorderly, hardscrabble Waxhaw backcountry of South Carolina colony, in the seventh year of the reign of King George III.

# 1

## A Roaring Fellow

Jackson's rise to fortune and then fame was unparalleled among the major political leaders of his generation. A few of the others could claim they had made their own way. Jackson's close ally Martin Van Buren was the son of a rural New York tavern keeper, and moved up the ladder of the law and politics by dint of his diligence, charm, and ability to make useful connections. Jackson's adversary Henry Clay, although born in comfortable circumstances in Virginia and trained in the law by Thomas Jefferson's old mentor George Wythe, was, like Jackson, an adoptive westerner, having moved to Kentucky to establish his name. But none of these men had to climb nearly as much or as hard as did Jackson.

Jackson's early life was even more dissimilar from those of the presidents who preceded him. It is often noted that Jackson was the first backcountry president, a product of the Carolina mountains who later moved to a state that lay entirely to the west of the Appalachians. Jackson's western background, though, was not the only thing that set him apart. With the exception of John Adams, the son of a Quincy, Massachusetts, farmer and shoemaker, no president before him was reared in anything resembling a commoner's family—and even Adams's father had had the wherewithal to send his boy to Harvard. Compared to the wellborn slaveholders Washington, Jefferson, Madison, and Monroe, or to John Adams's fortunate son John Quincy, Jackson came into the world a perfect nobody.

American success of Jackson's magnitude has always had its perils. Jackson suffered from the sting of snobbery, and had to overcome the awkwardness that any outsider feels among insiders. He also suffered, especially during his service as a boy soldier in the Revolution, searing personal losses and indignities that would mark him for life and make him highly sensitive about any perceived slight. But those same experiences helped instill in Jackson his democratic sensibilities, his mistrust of political privilege, and his avowed dedication to the egalitarian ideals of 1776. Although he would master the gentleman's code of etiquette, and though he gained a great deal of money and power, he would never delude himself, or try to delude others, that he had been to the manor born. The only delusion was the one held by those who prejudged him as a backwoods barbarian, lacking the education and refined virtue required to lead the nation.

In the winter of 1767, Andrew Jackson, a Carolina small farmer— the father of two young sons with another child well on the way— unexpectedly perished. There are stories about his being crushed by a log while clearing timber, but nobody knows for certain what happened. Jackson and his family, immigrants from the north of Ireland, had been living in America for less than two years. His third son and namesake, born on March 15, began life surrounded by death and grief.

The late Andrew had taken his wife, Elizabeth, and their boys, Hugh and Robert, out of Ulster at the tag end of a long migration wave to America caused by crop failures, rising rents, and an uprooting of the tenant farmer population. Rather than depend on wage work in the Ulster woolen and linen trades—both Andrew and Elizabeth had been linen weavers—a quarter of a million Scots-Irish wound up crossing the Atlantic during the decades from 1700 until the outbreak of the American Revolution. By the time the Jacksons arrived, most of the worthwhile land in the immigrants' favored destination, Pennsylvania, had been bought up or leased out. After traveling down the Great Wagon Road that led into the

Carolina backcountry, the family found a small available tract near Twelve Mile Creek in the scrub-pine Catawba River Valley, familiarly known as the Waxhaw settlement. It had been named after its native Indian population, which had been almost completely wiped out before 1765, killed by disease and in combat with the colonists.

Straddled across the North and South Carolina border—there are still disputes about which province was young Andrew's birthplace—the Waxhaw district and the surrounding backcountry displayed a mixture of disorder, clannishness, and piety. Distant from the burgeoning rice and tobacco plantations of the seacoast, lacking political power and government protection, the residents heeded private codes of justice, reciprocity, and retribution. A war between settlers and Cherokee raiders in 1760 had caused intense turmoil, from which the district was still recovering when the Jacksons arrived. A crime wave in the middle of the decade led more substantial farmers in South Carolina to form vigilante committees and roust the suspected lower-class evildoers. Farmers in Anson, Orange, and Rowan counties in North Carolina, adjoining the Waxhaw area, began agitating in 1764 against corrupt officials, royalist tax and fee collectors, and inadequate representation in the colonial assembly. Petitions from self-styled "poor industrious peasants" for relief and reform from the colonial legislature gave way to the terrorizing of state officers, disruption of court proceedings, and other militant protests, until a combination of colonial militia and royal troops, on orders of the royal governor, crushed the uprising in 1771.[1]

The political upheaval deepened the region's cultural insularity. The Scots-Irish, who quickly asserted their domination over the district, settled in family groups. (The Jacksons lived within a few miles of Elizabeth's five married sisters and another family of in-laws.) Turning inward, the settlers' chief source of spiritual order and community life was the local Presbyterian church, which, though small and rude by eastern standards, was the most substantial place of worship in the region and was pastored by an educated clergyman. The congregation held to a strict and severe Calvinist faith, God-fearing, fatalistic, and far removed from the High Church Anglicanism that was officially established in both North and South Carolina colonies.

Elizabeth Jackson's piety, along with her family ties, helped her weather the sudden loss of her husband. James Crawford, her sister Jane's husband, lived seven miles from the Jacksons' log cabin homestead, on a comparatively large and fertile tract worked by a number of slaves.* The Crawfords took in Elizabeth and the boys for good. In return, Elizabeth would oversee the running of the household—her sister was an invalid—and supervise the raising of the Crawfords' eight children as well as her own. Elizabeth decided that her baby, Andrew, was special, and that he would become a minister of God. She scraped together what money she could to ensure that he would receive the best schooling from two nearby clergymen. She dreamed he would be spared the drudgery and eternal obscurity of his father and the great majority of backcountry migrants and become an honorable leader of his community.

The scraps of evidence about Jackson's boyhood show he was a sickly but high-spirited youngster. A surviving slave from the Crawford home named Aunt Phyllis, interviewed decades later, said he suffered from a malady she called the Big Itch, and that he was the most mischievous boy in the neighborhood. Although sent to a religious academy that was a cut above the local field school, Jackson's attitude toward religion remained indifferent, and his formal studies never took hold beyond some basic lettering and arithmetic. (His spelling would always be atrocious.) Andrew grew to be slightly over six feet tall, spindly and angular, with a thick thatch of sandy red hair. His speech—especially when he flew into one of his frequent shouting rages—was wrapped in an Ulster brogue.

The Revolution cut short Jackson's youth when he was barely in his teens. The war hit the Waxhaw settlement hard, pitting local

---

*Andrew was most likely born at the Crawford home, on the South Carolina side of the boundary, although a strong oral tradition claims the birth occurred at George McCamie's cabin nearby, which was in North Carolina. Jackson considered himself a native South Carolinian.

patriots against their Tory neighbors as well as against British troops. All three of the Jackson boys saw active service. Andrew's eldest brother, Hugh, died of exposure following the Battle of Stono Ferry in 1779. The younger two Jacksons served in the Continental Army, Andrew as a courier; both witnessed (and Robert fought in) the furious Battle of Hanging Rock in October 1780, which forced a British outpost to retreat to nearby Camden but cost the Americans heavy casualties. Six months later, betrayed by a Waxhaw loyalist, the Jackson brothers fell into the hands of British troops. After the boot-cleaning and slashing incident (in which Robert also was maimed), the young captives were placed under royal guard at the Camden city jail, where they were surrounded by more than two hundred other injured and wasted prisoners, and given little food and no medical attention. Smallpox broke out and both brothers contracted it.

Elizabeth Jackson, distraught but daring, traveled to Camden and managed to arrange for the release of her sons as part of an exchange for some captured British soldiers. Robert died two days later; Andrew lingered on in a delirious fever. Elizabeth nursed him, and the fever broke, but before her son had fully recovered, she learned that several other Waxhaw patriots, including two of her nephews, were being held aboard a pestiferous prison ship in Charleston harbor. Bound by her clan obligations, she journeyed the 160 miles to Charleston and gained admission to the ship—but before long she too died, of cholera. Local relatives buried her in an unmarked grave in an open field. Some time later, according to one family story, a sorry bundle of Elizabeth's clothing arrived back in Waxhaw district and was delivered to her sole surviving son, who was still recovering from his near demise.

"When the tidings of her death reached me I at first could not believe it," Jackson later recalled, "when I finally realized the truth I was utterly alone, and tried to recall her last words to me."[2]

It is easy to imagine that severe feelings of confusion, guilt, persecution, and rage, as well as loneliness, gripped the orphan. What is clear is that Jackson, at fifteen, affected the quarrelsome, reckless bravado of a bereft adolescent, desperately searching. Once he had recovered from his illness, he fell back on the generosity of his Waxhaw kin, but he found them peremptory and they found him incorrigible. He moved in with a neighbor and worked for the man's son, a saddler, but was more interested in racehorses and the sporting life than in learning a trade. His prospects briefly brightened in 1783 when he received word that one of his Irish grandfathers had left him an inheritance of four hundred pounds—a sum that, in steadier hands, might have provided the ample beginnings of a new life as an independent farmer. When Jackson arrived in Charleston, though, he squandered the money, acting out the role of a low-country gentleman rake, buying himself a brace of pistols, a gold watch, fine clothes, and a splendid horse, and spending what was left on a bender of gambling, drinking, and women. Only a lucky roll of the dice, on which he had wagered his new horse, enabled him to pay off his debts and return, shamefaced, to the Waxhaw settlement.

Jackson was never really able to reconnect with his older relatives, whose refusal to let him live down his Charleston spree reinforced his obstreperousness. He taught school, then went back to work for the saddler, boarding with one neighbor after another, thoroughly miserable. Yet Jackson was also chastened enough to lay aside part of his earnings and plan on making something of himself. In 1784, he left the Waxhaw district permanently, traveling north to Salisbury, North Carolina, with the intention of studying the law. Jackson's mind and his habits remained unsettled; one local later recalled he was "the most roaring, rollicking, game-cocking, horse-racing, card-playing, mischievous fellow that ever lived" in the town—and the best lawyer in the area refused to take him on as an apprentice.[3] But Jackson picked up enough of the law from other local attorneys to qualify for the bar in September 1787. When the job of public prosecutor in newly settled middle Tennessee opened up, one of his fellow apprentices, a drinking friend with political connections (who had been named to the Tennessee district superior court), got him appointed. While traveling west, Jackson purchased his first slave, a woman not much older than he, and, taking offense from a fellow lawyer, fought the first of what would be his numerous duels, this one bloodless—in both instances staking his claim as a southern gentleman. In October 1788, aged twenty-one, he arrived in Nashville, his grievous losses and self-inflicted setbacks seemingly overcome.

Jackson's rapid rise bespoke social and political as well as personal changes. The winning of independence had hastened white migration west of the Appalachians, pushing past the pre-Revolutionary settlements along the rivers of eastern Tennessee all the way to the Cumberland River region and beyond. The uprooting of the old Tory elite of the colonial North Carolina bench and bar had also opened up a vocation much better suited to Jackson's talents and temperament than the ministry or saddle making. As one of the first lawyers to arrive in the Cumberland, Jackson quickly became one of Nashville's leading citizens in the years immediately preceding Tennessee's attainment of statehood.

Jackson made the most of his opportunities. In 1791, he secured his social and political stature with his successful courtship of Rachel Donelson, a plain but warmhearted daughter of a prominent local clan. Rachel had been wed to one Lewis Robards, but the marriage had broken down; two years after the Jacksons wed, they learned that the divorce Robards had supposedly obtained was not yet final. Although many of the details remain obscure, Andrew and Rachel had to submit to the humiliation of a second exchange of vows, and the charge that she was a bigamist would come back to haunt Jackson in later years. But it was thanks largely to his Donelson ties that the young lawyer found a home and became a protégé of the most powerful man in Nashville, territorial governor William Blount. With Blount's patronage, Jackson climbed the ladder of law and politics, becoming attorney general in 1791 and winning election to the Tennessee state constitutional convention in 1795. When Tennessee formally gained statehood in 1796, and the legislature chose Blount to be one of its two U.S. senators, Blount anointed Jackson to be the state's first congressman and the voters affirmed his choice. A year later, when the Senate ousted Blount on charges that he was planning a military intrigue against Spanish Florida, the Tennessee legislature named Jackson as his replacement.

Congressman and then Senator Jackson was a decided and, to some, bizarre outsider during his time in Philadelphia, the nation's capital. To the fastidious, he looked and acted uncivilized: "Queue down his back tied with an eel skin," the refined Jeffersonian Albert Gallatin recalled. "Dress singular. . . . Manners those of a rough backwoodsman."[4] Gallatin exaggerated Jackson's coarseness, but the Tennessean certainly lacked the suaveness, patience, and oratory required of a successful legislator. The slight impression he did make in the House showed his views were firmly in line with those of the rapidly organizing Jeffersonian opposition to President George Washington's Federalist administration. Jackson opposed the Jay Treaty, ratified a year earlier, for its alleged favoritism to the British, especially in acceding navigation rights on the Mississippi River. In a debate over direct federal taxation, he supported taxing slaves as well as land, on the grounds that excluding slaves would have shown partiality to the wealthy. His only notable speech was a brief defense of western military preparedness against the Indians. He joined with a handful of other congressmen in repudiating a fawning resolution praising the entire Washington administration on the occasion of Washington's retirement—a vote, his biographer James Parton wrote, that marked him as a member of "the most radical wing of the Jeffersonian party, the 'Mountain' of the House of Representatives."[5] Jackson also kindled friendships with the New York opposition leader Edward Livingston and with William Duane, the fiery editor of the anti-administration newspaper the *Aurora*, who would be prosecuted by the John Adams administration under the repressive alien and sedition laws.

In April 1798, after serving just over six months in the Senate, and with another Blount loyalist waiting in the wings, Jackson resigned, returned to Tennessee, and took up an appointment as a circuit-riding justice of the state's superior court. He enjoyed dispensing justice and, by all accounts, was good at it; and his salary of six hundred dollars per year was second only to the state governor's. But Rachel grew weary of his extended absences, and the pay, although generous, was insufficient to enable Jackson to pay off his debts and live as a country gentleman. During his rise to respectability, he had invested heavily in planting, merchandising, and land speculation—but had lost almost everything in 1795 when a business associate whose notes he had endorsed went bankrupt. Forced to start over again on a new parcel of land outside Nashville, he gradually made his way back by carefully managing his credit, buying slaves, and investing in the growing boom market for short-staple cotton, now easily processed thanks to Eli Whitney's cotton gin. In 1804, he stepped down from the court to tend to his growing enterprise, which he called the Hermitage, and which in time would become one of the larger cotton-growing plantations in Tennessee. For the rest of his life Jackson would be the slaveholding master of his own estate (which he would always call his "farm"); and he had acquired an undying distrust of banks, paper money, and, above all, debt.

But Jackson's deepest passion was for the military. Shortly after he arrived in Tennessee, he had secured, through his political connections, the job of judge advocate of the Tennessee militia. A fire-eating hater of unyielding Indians, he began angling to be named major general of the militia as soon as he returned from Congress, and finally won the post in 1802. Thereafter, his involvement in politics and the law dwindled and his military ambitions soared—which resulted in new frustrations. For a decade, he thrilled at any sign that war might be declared, if not against the British then against their allies, the Spanish and the Indians. (Jackson took a kinder view of the French, sharing in the early misimpression, common enough among backcountry Republicans, that, as he wrote, "the conquering arm of Bonaparte" was spreading "the rights of man" across a benighted Old World.)[6] But with Presidents Jefferson and Madison responding to British provocations with commercial sanctions, there was little need for anyone's military services, least of all the untested Jackson's.

So it was that in 1805, Jackson fell in with the wandering adventurer, former vice president Aaron Burr, and became a secondary agent of Burr's mysterious plans to head an ill-defined military expedition against the Spanish. Some of the facts of Jackson's involvement are murky, like everything else connected to the Burr conspiracy. Burr was highly popular in Nashville, not least for his strong support of Tennessee statehood a decade earlier. His killing of Alexander Hamilton in 1804 had only enhanced his reputation in the heavily Republican state, where dueling was a gentleman's prerogative. When Burr visited the Cumberland on an exploratory visit, Jackson hosted him, and before long he agreed to provide officers and matériel should a patriotic war with Spain arise. Burr's chief confederate, the erratic but inveterate schemer James Wilkinson, fearing that he might be accused of treason, suddenly alerted President Jefferson to Burr's plan. Jefferson ordered Burr's arrest, at which point Jackson backed off. Jackson offered his services to Secretary of War Henry Dearborn. Dearborn, wary, turned him down; Jackson, offended, went back to defending Burr as a maligned innocent. Burr's acquittal in the spring of 1807 gave Jackson a measure of vindication, but no glory. (It also fueled his hatred of Wilkinson, whom he blamed for turning the plan into an illicit venture and then dishonorably saving his own skin.) Jackson returned to the Hermitage, purchased additional land and slaves, and gambled on his gamecocks and racehorses. He rebutted charges of misconduct stemming from a duel in 1806, in which he had killed young Charles Dickinson, reputedly the best shot in Tennessee, over some drunken remarks Dickinson had made about Rachel Jackson. Protective, proud, and insecure, Jackson clung to his military commission—a self-made southwestern planter in his early forties, restlessly hoping for a war.

War finally came in 1812. Jackson's mightiest enemies, the British, refused to end their forceful restriction of American shipping, and President Madison and the Republican congressional majority believed nothing short of war could uphold the nation's sovereignty. Yet it would be more than a year before Jackson saw consequential action, mainly because the early fighting concentrated on the northern theater, including the humiliating surrender of Detroit without a shot to the British in August 1812. Early in January 1813, Jackson led an army of over two thousand Tennessee volunteers toward New Orleans, to help defend the lower Mississippi Valley. By the time the Tennesseans reached Natchez, however, President Madison's new secretary of war, John Anderson, aborted the mission and ordered Jackson to dismiss his troops. Thwarted and furious, Jackson halted, but he refused to disband his forces, which would have left them under the command of none other than his despised foe James Wilkinson. (After narrowly escaping a court-martial conviction in connection with the Burr conspiracy, Wilkinson retained his commission, and had been temporarily restored to his former posting in New Orleans.) Instead, Jackson led his troops on a difficult march all the way back to Nashville. The toughness he displayed on the trek home earned Jackson a nickname from his foot soldiers, "Hickory," possibly referring to the hard-shelled nuts of the trees so plentiful in Tennessee, possibly to the durable wood itself; the name soon mutated into "Old Hickory." But the only fighting he saw early in the war was an armed brawl with the brothers Jesse and Thomas Hart Benton in a Nashville hotel bar, over yet another conflict of manly honor. The fracas left Jackson with a serious pistol wound in the shoulder, from which he nearly died. The latter Benton, then a military aide, would wind up in Missouri and, after his own circuitous political journey, become one of President Jackson's staunchest allies.

In the autumn, Jackson finally received the orders he had long awaited. Along the Gulf of Mexico lay the disputed territory of West Florida. The Americans claimed it was theirs under the terms

of the Louisiana Purchase of 1803, but the Spanish had held on and
maintained a garrison in the vital port of Mobile. At the outbreak of
the war with Britain, military officials worried greatly that Spain,
reinforced by Indian allies, might enter the conflict against the
United States. An American show of force in April 1813, led by
General Wilkinson, pushed the Spanish out of Mobile, but the
Indian threat remained. Jackson's job was to contain it—and he
rose to the task with all of his pent-up personal ambition and
nationalist zeal.

The vast majority of southwestern Indians, numbering about
twenty thousand, lived peaceably under treaties with the United
States. They included approximately two thousand Muskogees—
called "Creeks" by the Americans because of their skill in traversing
and settling in the heavily creek-crossed terrain—in Georgia and in
southern Alabama, which was then part of Mississippi Territory. In
northern Alabama, however, Chief Red Eagle led approximately
four thousand combative Creeks known as Red Sticks, for the deco-
rative paint they applied to their bodies and war clubs. The son of a
Scots trader, Red Eagle (named William Weatherford in English)
had chosen his mother's family over his father's. In 1811, he was
stirred when the charismatic northern Shawnee warrior Tecumseh
visited him with plans to form a great pan-tribal Indian confederation that would end the white men's remorseless encroachments.
Red Eagle's commitment to Tecumseh was sealed in December
1811 when a great earthquake hit the southern states; he viewed it
as an omen. It would mean breaking with older Creek chieftains as
well as defying other tribes who were counseling accommodation.
Late in 1812, the slaughter of two white families by some Red
Sticks sparked a civil war among the Creeks, as well as a war
between the Red Sticks and the settlers.

It was the massacre of Fort Mims along the Alabama River that
prompted Jackson and the Americans to intervene. In 1813, a
group of settlers, having botched an attack on a Red Sticks raiding
party, took refuge at the fort, which was little more than a stockade
surrounding a trading post run by the part-Indian Samuel Mims.

The refugees joined three hundred white civilians and noncombatant Indians, probably an equal number of slaves, and 120 militiamen. On August 30, a thousand Red Sticks, commanded by Red Eagle and yet another part-Indian named Paddy Welsh, overcame the Americans' feeble defenses, set fire to the fort, clubbed the American senior officer to death, then systematically butchered the white inhabitants. Red Eagle, no stranger to the terrors of frontier warfare but sickened at the mayhem, tried to halt it, and was forcibly restrained by his own men. White children reportedly had their brains splattered against the fort's stockade; pregnant women, it was said, were sliced open and their fetuses ripped from their wombs; scalping was widespread. Only the blacks were, for the most part, spared, so that the attackers could use them as slaves.

Reports of the Mims atrocities aroused Jackson's ire against all Indians who would not submit to American domination. Worse, Red Eagle's alliance with Tecumseh, who had since allied with the British, raised in Jackson's mind the specter of an enormous ruthless army of "savages" and redcoats rampaging across the American mainland. Ordered by Tennessee's governor to take the offensive, Jackson assured the peaceable Creeks and their leaders that he would defend them, but vowed personal revenge against the Red Sticks. "With his soldiers," Jackson told his men, "[your general] will face the danger of the enemy; and with them he will participate [in] the glory of a conquest."[7] At the Creek village of Tallushatchee, south of Huntsville, Alabama, one thousand of Jackson's troops encircled nearly two hundred Red Sticks, slaughtered every one of them in a revolting scene of fire and blood, and marched the village's women and children back to Jackson's camp as captives. (American losses totaled five dead and forty-one wounded.) "We have retaliated for the destruction of Fort Mims," Jackson reported curtly to Tennessee governor William Blount. "We shot them like dogs," a then-unknown Tennessee soldier and marksman named David Crockett later recollected.[8]

In early November, Jackson won another huge victory at the village of Talladega, using the same tactics of encirclement, feint, and merciless counterattack. (At least three hundred Red Sticks died, while American losses amounted to fifteen killed and eighty-six wounded.) But Jackson had erred in his logistics, leading his troops into remote terrain where supplies came only from unreliable contractors. Jackson was reduced to arguing with his starving militiamen, on one occasion threatening violence, in order to prevent desertions. Even when fresh meat arrived on hoof, his men remained sullen. Only the fortuitous arrival of eight hundred volunteer replacements, further reinforced in March by twenty-five hundred fresh Tennessee militiamen, permitted Jackson to remain in the field. At the end of March, Jackson's forces, now numbering close to four thousand men including Creek and Cherokee allies, overwhelmed nearly a thousand Red Sticks at Horseshoe Bend in another bloodbath. Three weeks later, Red Eagle surrendered. Some undaunted Red Sticks joined forces with the British in East Florida, but the remainder of the Creek Nation submitted to Jackson.

As his price for defeating the rebellion and settling the civil war among the Creeks, Jackson, acting on the authority of President Madison, imposed a treaty that ceded 23 million acres of the Indians' lands to the United States—more than half of the Creeks' total holdings, representing approximately three-fifths of the present-day state of Alabama and one-fifth of Georgia. The forfeited lands included territories held by Creeks who had resisted Red Eagle—many of whom had fought alongside Jackson—as well as territories held by Red Sticks. With this agreement, Jackson believed, the Creeks would never again pose a military threat to the United States. The treaty also completed a land grab that opened immense tracts of exceptionally fertile and long-coveted soil to American speculators and farmers.

The government rewarded Jackson for his success with a commission as major general in the U.S. Army. Jackson had suffered during the Creek campaign: his health, already damaged by his dueling wounds (and especially by Jesse Benton's pistol shot), had been permanently broken by the chronic dysentery he had con-

tracted during the fighting. Unable to digest food, he had sometimes subsisted on nothing more than diluted gin. But the haggard
Jackson could now boast of a superior national military appointment, and, with that, the beginnings of a national reputation.

In strictly military terms, that reputation was overblown. Jackson's triumphs over the Creeks—and, indeed, the very existence of
his army—had been endangered by the supply shortages at his base
camp. His foe, although formidable, was far less so than the well-
equipped British army and navy. The Red Sticks had had only limited contacts with white settlers, and were ill prepared to undertake
a full-scale woodlands war against the Americans. Lacking mus-
ketry and ordnance, they proved to be easy targets whenever Jackson was able to outnumber them, which Jackson regularly proved
capable of doing. Jackson did perform well on the field for an inex-
perienced commander, deploying his men skillfully and redeploy-
ing them swiftly in the heat of battle. His indomitable will,
displayed both in suppressing mutiny among the militia and in dictating peace to the surrendering Creek chiefs, overcame his own
torments.

By crushing the Creeks, Jackson achieved in the Deep South and
Southwest a victory that, in the long run, proved the equivalent of
General William Henry Harrison's earlier removal of Tecumseh and
the Indian threat in the Northwest at the Battle of the Thames in
October 1813. Given the delicate balance of American victories
and debacles in the War of 1812, it made Jackson look like a military genius. But the reality was more prosaic: Jackson, when provoked, was an unterrified and accomplished killer.

The Indian threat routed, Jackson turned his full fury against the
British, who, the Americans calculated, were planning an invasion
somewhere along the Gulf coast. After repulsing a British attack on
Mobile, Jackson made war against the Spanish in West Florida who,
in conjunction with the British (he told Rachel), were "arming the
hostile Indians to butcher our women & children."[9] The only snag was

that the United States was not formally at war with Spain. Caring little for technicalities, Jackson threatened to invade Florida; the alarmed Spanish governor invited the British to land at Pensacola, in violation of Spanish neutrality. Now fully justified in his own mind, Jackson invaded, seized Pensacola, rendered it militarily useless, then gave it back to the Spanish. A week later, Jackson learned that the British had launched an invasion force from Jamaica, numbering about ten thousand troops and sixty ships, aimed at New Orleans—and that he had been placed in charge of the city's defense. He fortified the existing American defenses at Mobile, and then scrambled two thousand soldiers in nine days, arriving with about seven hundred troops in a jumpy city that was unprepared for battle.

The war had entered a critical phase. A British diversionary force had burned Washington in early August and sent Madison and his cabinet scurrying into the Virginia night. But American militiamen somehow succeeded in halting the British advance at Baltimore. In Anglophilic, Federalist New England, where the war had always been deeply unpopular, there was open talk of secession and pursuing a separate peace; antiwar dissenters planned a convention to meet at Hartford, Connecticut, in mid-December. Across the Atlantic, in the Flemish town of Ghent, an American delegation, including John Quincy Adams, lately the American minister to St. Petersburg, and Henry Clay, had undertaken peace talks with the British, but was running into diplomatic roadblocks. News traveled slowly, and it was impossible to know whether an honorable settlement, continued military stalemate, or national dissolution was in the offing.

New Orleans was an entryway to the immense territories obtained in the Louisiana Purchase, the bulwark of what Thomas Jefferson had envisaged as an American empire of liberty. If the British could seize the city, they would control the entire lower Mississippi Valley—and, if they linked up with royal forces sent from Canada, they would then effectively control all of what was then the American West. As the British government had never recognized the Spanish retrocession of these western lands to the French in 1800, the invaders could claim that the entire Louisiana Purchase had been illegitimate and that, by right of conquest, the land belonged to Britain. But regardless of such scheming, possession of New Orleans was crucial to the outcome of the current fighting. Should the Americans lose the city—and if no settlement was forthcoming at Ghent—they would almost certainly lose the war. And although New Orleans, surrounded by lakes and bayous, enjoyed formidable natural protections against invasion, the American situation there was highly uncertain.

Louisiana had been admitted to the Union in 1812, but New Orleans, with its long-resident Creole French and Spanish populations, could not be counted on for undivided loyalty and support. South of the city, control of the bayous around Barataria Bay belonged to a band of well-armed privateers and smugglers, commanded by the Haitian-born Jean Laffite, whose only loyalties were to themselves. As in any southern state, there were fears of slave unrest. In January 1811, then territorial governor W. C. C. Claiborne had ruthlessly suppressed a rebellion of upwards of five hundred slaves, who burned several sugarcane plantations north of New Orleans and briefly menaced the city itself. Now, with a British armada at Louisiana's doorstep, there was reason to fear that the invaders would mobilize the bondsmen.

On December 13, scouts spotted the British invaders proceeding from the Gulf of Mexico toward Lake Borgne, just west of the city. Three days later, Jackson declared martial law in New Orleans. His own command still numbered, at most, seven hundred, and there was no sign that reinforcements would arrive before the British did, and so the American general improvised. Upon arriving in New Orleans Jackson had sneered at the Baratarians as "hellish banditti," but now he struck an alliance with Laffite. Over the objections of local slaveholders, Jackson also organized two battalions of free black soldiers; and a small contingent of loyal Creek Indians also joined the American side. Finally, on December 20, Jackson's old friend General John Coffee arrived with a little more than six hundred veterans, including cavalry; the next day, fourteen hundred Tennessee recruits under another old friend, newly elevated Major General William Carroll, marched into town, as did more than one hundred Mississippi dragoons under Major Thomas Hinds. As they swarmed through the streets of New Orleans, the Americans at least resembled a credible fighting force. But unlike his forays against the Creeks, Jackson would have to fight a defensive battle—and this time his army would be gravely outnumbered.

On December 23, Jackson received two agitated Creole messengers who informed him that the British were closing in without resistance. Jackson calmly offered his visitors some wine, thanked them for their intelligence, and then reportedly swore: "I will smash them, so help me God!"[10] Jackson redeployed his main force five miles east of the city, behind an old millrace. The British repeatedly bombarded Jackson's forces in an effort to soften them up. Dug in behind mud ramparts, sugar barrels, and cotton bales, the Americans, aided by fire from the *Louisiana*, a ship anchored in the Mississippi, withstood the assaults. By the morning of January 8, more than two thousand additional Kentucky militiamen had arrived, although only one-third of them carried guns. Jackson now had about four thousand men on his front line with only about another thousand in reserve. Less than a mile to the east were three columns of British regulars and a regiment of conscripted West Indians—a grand total of more than five thousand troops, most of them hardened veterans of the Napoleonic Wars, with another five thousand held in reserve. Their commander was Lieutenant General Sir Edward Pakenham, brother-in-law of the Duke of Wellington. At dawn, a British Congreve rocket soared above a cypress swamp to the left of Jackson's line, signaling the start of Pakenham's assault.

The Americans were lucky as well as skillful. Pakenham had hoped to seize the opposite bank of the Mississippi, outflank Jackson, and pin down the Americans with crossfire. But the river would not cooperate, and plans to ferry over fifteen hundred troops in barges had to be drastically scaled back. Meanwhile, the British Forty-fourth Regiment, led by Lieutenant Colonel Thomas Mullens, was positioned to spearhead the British attack by carrying ladders and sugarcane bundles that the main force would later use to scale Jackson's breastworks. Only when Mullens's men were in attack position did they realize that they had left the ladders and cane bundles behind. By the time the redcoats retrieved their equipment, the battle was well under way.

Despite these mishaps, some major deployment errors by Jackson might still have handed victory to the British. Although a smaller number than Pakenham had expected, five hundred British troops under Colonel William Thornton did cross over to the western bank of the Mississippi, and easily dispersed the token American defense force (its weakness the result of what might have been a critical misjudgment on Jackson's part). Thornton's men rushed to the American batteries where they could rake Jackson's troops undisturbed. But Thornton's men had actually landed well to the south of where they had intended, and arrived in position too late in the battle. On the eastern bank of the river, meanwhile, Jackson had left the American line nearest the Mississippi vulnerable, and early in the fighting a brigade of the Ninety-third Highlanders, commanded by Colonel Robert Rennie, managed to gain the top of the ramparts overlooking the canal. American artillery and marksmen let loose a volley that cut down Rennie's front ranks (including Rennie himself), but the rest of the Ninety-third's column, under Major General John Keane, might easily have breached Jackson's line. Instead of following Rennie's lead, however, Keane's Highlanders stuck to their original orders from Pakenham and veered toward the center of the field that lay before them. There, with their bagpipes blaring, they were butchered, along with Pakenham's main column. Behind their embankments, Jackson's motley collection of resisters—most effectively, twenty cannon crews—poured volleys of grape, canister, and rifle fire into the advancing enemy.

By eight in the morning, less than two hours after it had begun, the shooting stopped. Jackson walked from position to position congratulating the soldiers, as the army's band struck up "Hail Columbia." Then the Americans looked out over their fortifications.

The heaps of fallen British stretched out unbroken for as far as a quarter-mile. "The slaughter was shocking," John Coffee said after he had regained his composure. Eerily, while the battle smoke cleared off, there was a stirring among the slain soldiers, as redcoats who had used their comrades' bodies as shields began arising out of the gore. Even Jackson was shaken: "I never had so grand and awful an idea of the resurrection as on that day," he later recalled.[11] By one account, the British lost nearly three hundred killed and more than fifteen hundred wounded—all told, roughly 40 percent of Pakenham's attack force. American casualties that day totaled, according to Jackson's report, just thirteen killed and thirty-nine wounded. The disparity was almost impossible to comprehend.

As a strategist and tactician, Jackson had met his match in Sir Edward Pakenham. The Americans' slowness in massing their forces below New Orleans and their failure to secure the western bank of the Mississippi might easily have proved disastrous. Jackson, refusing to acknowledge any blunders on his own part, blamed the near-disaster on "[t]he want of discipline, the want of Order, a total disregard to Obedience, and a Spirit of insubordination" supposedly displayed by the beaten soldiers.[12] But Jackson's unswerving confidence had emboldened both the citizens of New Orleans and his own soldiers when they had seemed doomed. He had handled the fighting on the east bank expertly. Staving off the temptation to mount a risky counterattack, he had thrown the redcoats back to Lake Borgne. Two weeks after the battle, they headed back out to sea.

A month later, in early February, news of the outcome in New Orleans finally reached Washington—followed, just a bit more than a week later, by the news that on Christmas Eve, while Jackson's forces were digging in for combat, the British and Americans had signed a peace treaty in Ghent. By the time Jackson won his triumph, the war had been formally over for two weeks. Yet the irony did nothing to diminish the public exaltation. The dispatches first from Louisiana and then from Ghent undid the fractious New England Federalists, who had held their Hartford Convention and sent three envoys to lay their grievances before President Madison; forever after, Yankee Federalism would bear the taint of disloyalty. Unlike any other nation of the time, the United States had fought the British to a standstill. And the New Orleans battle made the ending of the war—an apparent stalemate, which, in the Ghent agreement, formally restored the status quo antebellum—look and feel like a huge American conquest, by affirming the Louisiana Purchase. Even before the Battle of New Orleans was over, the *Times* of London, informed of the Ghent treaty and reflecting on American military successes in 1814, complained that "[w]e have retired from the combat, with the stripes yet bleeding on our back." Jackson's astounding triumph placed a capstone on the Republic's moral victory.[13]

President Madison sent General Jackson a special commendation. Congress unanimously passed a lengthy resolution of thanks and ordered a gold medal be struck in his honor. The city of Washington, still climbing out of the ashes, erupted with delight, as did cities from Philadelphia to Nashville. Newspapers printed testimonials from Jackson's men attesting to their general's leadership and bravery.

Old Hickory, although a physical wreck, basked in the adulation. He had risen from next to nothing to become the most renowned American 'general since George Washington—the greatest hero of what some were calling the second American Revolution. He had wreaked his vengeance on the British army and their Indian and Spanish friends. As he neared the age of fifty, he knew he would have to sustain the honor he had won, lest his fame, unlike Washington's, disappeared. Like others plucked from obscurity, Jackson was unprepared for his apotheosis, and for having the stakes of his life suddenly rise even higher. Yet he did not turn away. Instead he understood his personal conquest as a New World republican triumph over Old World treachery and monarchism. "[T]he 8th of January," he proudly wrote to one associate a month after the battle, "will be ever recollected by the British nation, and always hailed by every true american." Jackson had undertaken a new vocation as a patriotic celebrity and, in time, democratic leader.[14]

2

---

# "Jackson and Reform"

For Andrew Jackson, the war never really ended. His defeat of the Creeks opened up millions of acres for white settlement, and his victory at New Orleans secured American dominion over the Mississippi Valley and much of the Gulf Coast. During the next seven years, Jackson further widened the opportunities for national expansion while leaving disturbing controversy in his wake. In 1822, after a brief retirement, he began what turned, a bit oddly, into a serious campaign for the presidency, and went on to win two years later what he and his supporters believed was a crushing popular triumph—only to be thwarted when the House of Representatives decided the election in favor of Jackson's erstwhile ally Secretary of State John Quincy Adams.

Jackson ascribed his defeat to malevolent forces, headed by Henry Clay of Kentucky, who were determined to restore the spirit of aristocracy. Jackson would make routing those forces, and reclaiming the office he thought rightfully his, the basis for a new presidential campaign in 1828. He and his supporters were also able, as they had been four years earlier, to tap into a broader popular agitation that had arisen at the state and local levels in the aftermath of the war. This merging of Jackson's ambitions and resentments with what John C. Calhoun called "a general mass of disaffection to the Government" would make Jackson president—and create the foundations for the world's first modern democratic political party, the Jackson Democracy.[1]

• • •

After his remarkable triumph at New Orleans, General Jackson, now in command of the U.S. Army in the southern portion of the country, was responsible for shoring up the nation's southern border, threatened by restive Creeks, Cherokees, Choctaws, and Chickasaws as well as by the continuing Spanish possession of Florida. Despite opposition from Secretary of the Treasury William Crawford (who wanted to return large tracts Jackson had already obtained from the Indians), Jackson confronted tribal leaders and, in five separate treaties between 1816 and 1820, secured additional cessions totaling tens of millions of acres in what would eventually be five American states. In the third of these treaties, completed with the Cherokees in 1817, Jackson also undertook his first experiment with Indian removal. Acting under the assumption that Indians and whites would never peacefully coexist, Jackson arranged for the surrender of two million acres in Tennessee, Georgia, and Alabama, while setting aside the same amount of land, "acre for acre," west of the Mississippi River in Arkansas Territory for those Indians who wished to relocate. Although generally unpopular with the Cherokees, and obtained with bribes that even Jackson considered distasteful, the removal provisions seemed to work well for those individual Indians who were willing to leave. Over the next two years, six thousand Cherokees made the trek west, supplied by the American government with basic necessities (including a rifle) and transportation to their new homes.

By contrast, Jackson's actions against the Spanish, in what came to be known as the First Seminole War, caused an immediate storm. Once powerful and splendid, the Spanish empire in the Western Hemisphere had long been crumbling. Throughout Latin America, the Spanish crown was fighting what would finally prove, in the 1820s, to be lost causes against various wars of national independence. But in Florida, which they had reacquired from the British at the conclusion of the American Revolution and then retained under the Treaty of Ghent, the Spanish clung to power and caused considerable headaches for the Americans. Spanish control of Florida had always made the United States more vulnerable to attack and invasion from the Gulf of Mexico. Bands of Indians with settlements that straddled the Florida border—earlier dubbed Seminoles (or "separatists," in the Creek language) by the British—raided and harassed American settlements in south Georgia and escaped into Florida when the Americans pursued them. (American officials believed that the Spanish, goaded by British agents, were encouraging the attacks.) Alongside the Apalachicola River, sixty miles south of the American border, approximately 250 fugitive slaves had taken over an old British fort in 1815, providing an open invitation to other southwestern American slaves to run away.

With Spanish support, American troops destroyed the so-called Negro Fort and wiped out its inhabitants in July 1816, but the collaboration between the Spanish and the Americans ended there. Late in 1817, an American force laid waste to a Seminole settlement on American land after the local Seminole chief refused to yield. Nine days later, the Seminoles retaliated by virtually wiping out a party of fifty Americans (including soldiers, women, and children) traveling down the Apalachicola in an open boat. Hostilities continued, and in March 1818, Jackson and a three-thousand-man American army, under orders from President Monroe to subdue the Seminole threat and backed by two thousand Indian allies, invaded Florida, intending not merely to suppress the Seminoles but to expel the Spanish from the region for good. Jackson carried ambiguous authorization from President Monroe to provide "other services" in defense of "[g]reat interests."[2] Even without Monroe's go-ahead, though, Jackson had every intention of seizing Florida given the slightest opportunity to do so—one of the reasons, almost certainly, why Monroe placed him in charge of the mission.

Jackson's actions in Florida raised serious questions of propriety and, at times, legality. After marching to pick up supplies at the site of the Negro Fort, Jackson's forces drove eastward into the heart of Seminole territory, seized the Spanish fortress at St. Mary's, torched the large Seminole settlement of Bowlegs's town, and apprehended the two leading British agents in Florida, Robert Ambrister and

Alexander Arbuthnot. After a brief drumhead trial at St. Mary's, an officers' tribunal condemned the Britons to death for inciting the Indians. Jackson, meanwhile, headed west, with the ultimate objective of capturing the Spanish command center at Pensacola. Convinced, wrongly, that hostile Indians had gathered outside the city, Jackson and his troops arrived at the end of May to find it defended by a meager Spanish force whose resistance they briskly brushed aside. Jackson had promised, back in March, to complete his Florida campaign in sixty days. It took him slightly longer than that—but his triumph had come to include winning de facto American military control over all of Florida. And Jackson, flushed with victory, immediately announced he had even greater ambitions against Spain. If provided with additional troops, arms, and a frigate, he informed President Monroe at the beginning of June, "I will insure you Cuba" and further enlarge "the growing greatness of our nation."[3]

But Jackson was forced to repair back to the Hermitage instead of sailing to Santiago. He was suffering flare-ups from his old dueling wounds and from the dysentery he had contracted during the Creek campaign. While convalescing in Tennessee, he learned of a growing backlash in Washington against his Florida adventures. All along, the Spanish minister, Don Luis de Onís, had bitterly protested the American invasion. Only in early July, though, when President Monroe returned to the White House after a month-long absence, did the extent of the outrage inside the American government become apparent. Quietly—so quietly that Jackson actually regarded him as a supporter—Secretary of War John C. Calhoun charged that by seizing Pensacola, Jackson had declared war against Spain on his own, in flagrant violation of the Constitution, and that he deserved immediate censure. Secretary of the Treasury William H. Crawford went further, calling for the swift return of Florida to Spanish authority. Inside the cabinet, only Secretary of State John Quincy Adams defended Jackson's actions as a necessary extension of the campaign against the Seminoles. Thereafter, Adams, with exceptional diplomatic skill, would deflect objections to the American occupation and pave the way to America's purchase of Florida from Spain in the comprehensive Adams-Onís Transcontinental Treaty of 1819. Jackson, however, faced a congressional investigation into his conduct as commander, as well as a wider examination by a Senate committee of the entire American operation in Florida.

The results of the official inquiries were, for Jackson, bittersweet. After a prolonged debate (and with Jackson now in Washington to assist in his own defense), the House defeated all the resolutions brought against him over the seizure of Pensacola and the executions of Ambrister and Arbuthnot. The members also refused to call the capture of Florida unconstitutional. Yet in winning vindication, Jackson had to suffer through repeated public attacks on his integrity. One of the sternest of his critics, Speaker of the House Henry Clay, lambasted him for insubordination, and declared that approval of Jackson's reckless campaign would represent "a triumph of the military over the civil authority—a triumph over the powers of this house—a triumph over the constitution of this land." The Senate investigators, led by political friends of Secretary Crawford, delivered a calm and deliberate report that nevertheless ripped into Jackson, especially over the executions of the two British agents—"an unnecessary act of severity . . . and a departure from that mild and humane system . . . honorable to the national character."[4]

Jackson's accusers certainly had ulterior motives. Clay and Crawford were planning to run for the presidency, and found in Jackson's rise to public eminence a potential political threat as well as an appalling turn in American foreign and military policy. Yet the critics also scored damaging points. Without a formal declaration of war from Congress, Jackson's transformation of the conflict into a war against a Spanish colony lacked constitutional legitimacy, regardless of the congressional verdict in his favor (although, in fairness, President Monroe ought to have shared in the blame). Coming after the squelching of the immediate Seminole threat, the lightning-swift trial and execution of the two British agents served no clear military purpose, and had about it an air of cruel vengeance. But Jackson continued to regard these objections as trivial technicalities, given his sincere belief, shared by Secretary Adams and others, that the Indian menace would end only when the Spanish authority at Pensacola was broken.

Despite his formal exoneration, Jackson would never forget the sour aftermath of the Seminole War and the insults to his reputation. Neither would those Americans for whom Jackson, far from a betrayer of the Constitution, was a hero once again—a patriot who had given his all to protect ordinary American settlers from Indian attack and to uphold the national interest against corrupt, colonizing Old World monarchies, including the sly, ever-perfidious British. "Among the people," one Tennessee newspaper friendly to Jackson reported, ". . . his popularity is unbounded—old and young speak of him with rapture."[5]

While Congress was debating Jackson's alleged crimes, a financial panic leveled the American economy. Exacerbated by mismanagement and larceny by officers of the Second Bank of the United States, the crisis turned into the nation's first prolonged economic depression, and would not lift for four years. Congress, spurred by Secretary Crawford, responded with a retrenchment program that included reducing the size of the army by half and eliminating Jackson's generalship. Early in 1821, following the completion of Florida's transfer from Spanish to American authority, an embarrassed President Monroe offered Jackson the new post of governor of Florida Territory, which the sullen former general accepted. Jackson performed creditably, overseeing the establishment of territorial institutions and doing his best to integrate the larger Florida peninsula with the panhandle region, which the British had divided into West and East Florida. But the new governor also found himself quarreling with departing Spanish dons, fending off American speculators who descended on Pensacola, and facing difficulties in trying to arrange for the peaceable removal of the Seminoles. After eleven turbulent weeks, Jackson resigned and returned to the Hermitage.

Except for some strange turns of fortune, Old Hickory, the hero of New Orleans, now aged fifty-five, might have lived out his life as a Tennessee planter and a famous, if only to some, controversial old warrior. More adored than ever in his home state, Jackson turned aside an offer to run for governor, as he convalesced from the latest near-collapse of his health. He was more welcoming, however, when, in 1822, his powerful old Nashville political friends, now headed by the lawyer and land speculator John Overton, proposed to nominate him for the presidency as a stalking-horse candidate to fend off an opposing Tennessee faction led by one of Jackson's former army protégés, Governor William Carroll. Carroll and his adherents were friendly to Treasury Secretary Crawford—whom Jackson detested, and who was making an all-out effort for the presidency himself—and so Jackson joined in Overton's gambit. (Most of Jackson's Tennessee backers actually hoped that either John Quincy Adams or Henry Clay would win the election.) But Jackson's name proved magnetic to discontented politicians and voters far beyond Tennessee. Signs of widespread popular support, linked with Jackson's pride and his principles, propelled the supposed diversionary candidate into serious contention.

Banks and banking, more than the Indian threat, were on people's minds. Disputes over banks and paper money had already placed Jackson, despite his longtime friendships, directly at odds with the Overton men. Dating back to his near-ruination due to bad bank paper more than two decades earlier, Jackson harbored a deep distrust of banks and bankers. The Panic of 1819, which caused a prolonged controversy over state banking in Tennessee, intensified that distrust. In 1820, Jackson helped draft a public memorial that blamed the depression on "the large emissions of paper from the banks," and denounced efforts to meet the crisis with state-issued paper-money loans. The continuing efforts by the bank-friendly Overton faction to protect large debtors and state banks, and to expand credit-driven land speculation, enraged Jackson further. After the Tennessee legislature formally endorsed his presidential candidacy late in 1822, he began informing his closest supporters that he opposed all banks as a matter of principle. Overton, offended, tried to clip Jackson's wings by secretly supporting one of his and Jackson's old political enemies for election by the state legislature to the U.S. Senate in 1823. Getting wind of the scheme, Jackson allowed his supporters to place his own name in contention for the senate; after a furious, last-minute effort (in which Jackson himself turned up outside the legislature to present his case to individual lawmakers), Jackson won. While affirming he was dependent on no other man, Jackson showed that he possessed considerable political skills of his own.[6]

Suddenly, Jackson's presidential effort caught fire with the disaffected around the country. The disaffection had been building for several years. The glow of national ardor and unity that followed the conclusion of the War of 1812 had once augured what one Boston newspaper called an "era of good feelings"—but a series of shocks, at the state as well as the national level, had dissipated those feelings. Efforts to expand democratic political rights, including abolishing property requirements for voting, had been largely successful but had run into stiff resistance in numerous states, from Massachusetts to Virginia. Growing antislavery opinion in the North had sparked a crisis in 1819 over the admission of Missouri to the Union as a slave state, a crisis that raised the specter of national disunion until moderates led by Henry Clay hammered out an uneasy truce. The Panic of 1819 and ensuing depression worsened the political mood, directing popular anger at banks, especially the Second Bank of the United States, and at the well-connected politicians who had supported the banks' expansion.

The nation's political system came under extraordinary and completely unanticipated pressures. During the War of 1812, the old anti-Jeffersonian Federalist Party had collapsed as a national political force. With Federalism stigmatized as disloyal, especially after the New England Federalists' ill-fated, antiwar Hartford Convention, it seemed as if the Republican Party, under the leadership of President James Madison and his successor, James Monroe, would oversee a government unblemished by partisan divisions. But the class and sectional battles of the postwar era seemed to dash all hopes for unity, and there was a growing belief that the "one-party" Republicans had simply created a regime of insider corruption and manipulation. As Monroe's Secretary of War John C. Calhoun noted in 1820, the idea had arisen across the country that something was "radically wrong in the administration of the Government." Discontented Americans were "ready to seize upon any event and looking out anywhere for a leader." By 1823, Andrew Jackson appeared to be the leader they wanted.[7]

Each of Jackson's rivals for the presidency—John Quincy Adams, William H. Crawford, Henry Clay, and John C. Calhoun— had far greater government experience than he, though the antiestablishment mood made that as much of a political liability as a strength. Each also had a significant regional base of support, but lingering distrust from the crisis surrounding Missouri's statehood had eroded opportunities for each politician to reach beyond his respective region. Adams, the most distinguished of the contestants, could point to a long career of service in the Congress and in the diplomatic corps. He had renounced the Federalist Party nearly twenty years earlier, mitigating his association, strongest in the minds of older Jeffersonians, with his father's unpopular presidency. And Adams's brilliant tenure as secretary of state under Monroe made him Monroe's presumptive heir, especially as both Presidents Jefferson and Madison had been succeeded by their respective secretaries of state. Adams's major weakness was in the South where, following the Missouri crisis, planters were wary of supporting any Yankee, even though Adams, stifling his own antislavery views, had supported the extension of slavery into Missouri under the terms of Henry Clay's compromise.

Secretary of the Treasury Crawford had his own presumptions to the presidency, having backed off from challenging James Monroe in 1816 with an implicit understanding that he would receive the Republican nomination eight years later. Admired by orthodox Jeffersonians (including a young up-and-comer from New York, Senator

Martin Van Buren) for his retrenchment policies and support of limited government, Crawford, a Georgia cotton planter, generated little enthusiasm in antislavery New England and the expanding West, which was hungry for federal aid to transportation projects and other internal improvements. In contrast, Speaker of the House Clay was the outstanding western candidate, having devised a program combining internal improvements, a strengthened national bank, and protective tariffs for nascent manufacturers that was especially popular in the newer states from Ohio to Missouri. Clay hoped that by explaining the national benefits of his plan—which eventually came to be known as the American System—and by reminding voters of his role as peacemaker in the Missouri crisis, he could expand his support across the country. Finally, Secretary of War Calhoun, like Clay an ardent pro-improvement nationalist, sensed that neither Adams nor Clay could overcome Crawford's advantages in the Deep South, whereas he, a South Carolina slaveholder, could build a winning alliance of the South with pro-banking, pro-improvement interests in the Middle Atlantic states, above all in Pennsylvania.

Living up to its nickname, the "Keystone State," Pennsylvania proved to be the election's first important arena. Calhoun seemed assured of winning the state's support when its dominant "New School" Republican faction, eager to expand banking and economic improvement, backed him. But a revolt from below, led by the Philadelphia radical democrats William Duane and Stephen Simpson of the venerable Jeffersonian newspaper the *Aurora*, caught the Calhounites by surprise. Duane (whom Jackson had befriended thirty years earlier) and Simpson were the most vocal critics of the New School men and had turned fiercely against the existing paper-money and banking system (and especially against the Second Bank of the United States), charging that commercial banks exploited ordinary workingmen and farmers. Duane had long experience in electoral politics, dating back to the 1790s, and was an effective organizer; Simpson had served under Jackson at New Orleans and considered him the greatest man in America—the only candidate who would protect the interests of those Simpson called "the producing classes." Early in 1822, even before the Tennessee legislature had formally nominated Jackson, the *Aurora* floated his name as a possible presidential candidate. Two years later, after an exuberant statewide campaign that left the Calhounites grumbling about "grog shop politicians of the villages & the rabble of Pittsburgh and Philadelphia," the pro-Jackson forces captured control of the Pennsylvania nominating convention, thereby knocking Calhoun out of the race and giving Jackson's candidacy an enormous boost.[8]

William Crawford's campaign, meanwhile, was afflicted by cruel turns of fate. In September 1823, Crawford fell victim to what appears to have been a massive stroke, leaving him half blind and, for a time, immobile. Gamely, Crawford recovered enough strength to permit his supporters, led by Martin Van Buren, to carry on with their efforts. But Van Buren was counting on gaining Crawford the nomination through the traditional means of winning in the Republican congressional nominating caucus. Since 1796, this conclave of national party leaders had formally selected the Republican presidential candidate. By 1824, however, "King Caucus" had fallen into disrepute as a quasi-aristocratic anachronism. Local politicians and ordinary voters were demanding that the nominating power be transferred to state legislatures and nominating conventions, and in 1824, Adams, Clay, and Jackson chose to abstain from the congressional meeting. With only a tiny proportion of the Republican congressmen in attendance, Crawford won a lopsided and thoroughly Pyrrhic victory. Bearing the burden of what would turn out to be the last official caucus nomination cost him whatever slender possibility he still had of winning the presidency.

Building on their surging momentum, the Jackson forces promoted their man as the one truly national candidate, and the only contestant free of the insider clubbiness of official Washington. On the major issues, above all the protective tariff, Jackson took the same middle-of-the-road stance he had taken in the Senate, and presented it so artfully that his opponents charged him with two-faced obfuscation. More generally, the Jacksonians lamented a breakdown in national unity and national purpose, and hailed Jackson as a proven leader who would be "the President of the whole people, the enlightened ruler of an undivided empire, and not a sectional magistrate devoted to the 'universal Yankee nation' of the East or the mixed, mingled and confused population of the South." They also introduced various campaign innovations, including the mounting of frequent mass rallies and parades.[9]

With New England solid for Adams and the South divided between Crawford and Jackson, the Middle Atlantic states emerged as the essential battlegrounds. In New York (one of six states where the state legislature still chose presidential electors) the election-eering intrigues were, as ever, Byzantine. Crawford's lieutenant Martin Van Buren, unable to overcome a pro-Adams majority inside the legislature, did manage to suppress the vote for Clay, which would eventually prove crucial to the election's outcome. But the big turn occurred in Pennsylvania and New Jersey, where the voters, not the legislatures, chose the electors, and where Jackson won clear victories—in Pennsylvania by a huge margin. These results, combined with victories in North Carolina, Illinois, Indiana, and the new southwestern states of Alabama and Mississippi, as well as strong second-place finishes in Maryland, Ohio, and Missouri, proved that Jackson was the only candidate with strong support outside his regional base. All told, he had won 42 percent of the vote in the eighteen states where the voters chose electors— nearly 10 percentage points higher than his nearest competitor, Adams (who swept New England but won nowhere else).

Because of the multi-candidate field, however, Jackson was unable to secure the simple majority in the Electoral College required to win the presidency. The election would thus be settled by the House of Representatives. And under the Twelfth Amendment to the Constitution (ratified in response to the electoral deadlock between Thomas Jefferson and Aaron Burr in 1800), the House would decide from among the three top finishers, with each state delegation receiving one vote. The rules seemed favorable to Jackson. Thanks in part to Van Buren's manipulations in New York,

Clay had finished fourth and was thereby eliminated. All that stood between Jackson and the presidency, it seemed, were two supremely sectional candidates, Adams and Crawford—one a diplomat with limited experience in hard-knuckle electoral politics, the other a semi-blind hulk.

Considering how far Jackson had come in only two years, his run had been remarkable. A man of humble origins and minimal schooling, he had risen to win the backing of a broad cross section of the electorate for the highest office in the land. He had bested his sworn enemies from the Florida controversy, Henry Clay and William Crawford, further vindicating his patriotic honor. As president, in the words of one Pennsylvania supporter, he would cleanse "[t]he Giant Augean Stable at Washington" of insider corruption and sectional intrigue.[10]

Jackson did not, however, count on the continuing influence inside the House of Representatives of the resourceful also-ran Henry Clay, who, despite appearances, was down but far from out.

Clay believed that the election of Andrew Jackson would be disastrous, "the greatest misfortune that could befall the country." Reflecting on Jackson's Florida exploits, and on how military usurpation had played out in classical history, Clay told friends that the ex-general's elevation to the White House would "give the strongest guaranty that the republic will march in the fatal road which has conducted every other republic to ruin." Crawford was not much better in Clay's estimation, an enemy of public improvements who, in any event, was physically incapacitated—more so, Clay thought, than Crawford's stalwart supporters were conceding. That left Adams, whom Clay had long disliked (and with whom he had argued strenuously over the Transcontinental Treaty), but who at least shared Clay's nationalist, pro-improvement outlook. And so, Clay told associates in mid-December, he would throw his support to Adams, which would give the secretary of state virtually all the state delegations he needed to prevail in the House. On the evening of January 9, the two men met in Washington at Clay's

invitation, mainly, it seems, to smooth over their personal differences.[11]

The subsequent allegations that Adams and Clay struck a "Corrupt Bargain," in which Adams promised Clay the office of secretary of state in exchange for his support for the presidency, were
highly dubious—and also devastating. The only "proof" of the deal
came in the form of an unsubstantiated allegation printed in
Stephen Simpson's new and highly partisan Philadelphia newspaper, the *Columbian Observer.* The idea that sophisticated political
men such as Adams and Clay would strike an explicit bargain was
(and is) far-fetched. Clay was, in any case, a natural candidate for
the post, and would bring congressional influence, personal charm,
diplomatic experience, and geographic balance into the new administration, all of which Adams needed. Adams, with Clay's backing,
duly won the election in the House. Neither man thought it untoward when, two days later, Adams announced he had chosen Clay
to head the State Department—and neither thought it untoward
when Clay swiftly accepted.

It proved one of the greatest blunders in American political history. Clay and Adams may have sincerely believed that they acted
with perfect correctness, even statesmanship, in resolving the electoral stalemate. The Constitution had been followed to the letter.
Clay had backed the surviving presidential candidate with views
closest to his own. Adams then selected the man he thought best
suited to be his secretary of state. But apart from violating a universal political rule—that the appearance of wrongdoing can be just as
costly as actual wrongdoing—Clay and Adams flew in the face of
what were fast becoming the majoritarian, democratic imperatives
of American politics. In the House election, Clay had arranged for
his home state of Kentucky to vote for Adams—even though
Adams had not won a single popular vote there, and even though
the state legislature had instructed its congressmen to vote for the
second-place finisher, Jackson. Clay ignored Jackson's large plurality in the popular vote, his plurality in the Electoral College vote,
and the combination of first- and second-place finishes in the states

(which, if heeded, would have given Jackson a convincing majority in the House). As Adams came to realize, the outcome in the House lacked popular authority, "with perhaps two-thirds of the whole people adverse to the actual result." Privileged political insiders, it appeared, had triumphed over the people's voice.[12]

"So you see," Jackson thundered as soon as the controversy broke out, "the *Judas* of the West has closed the contract and will receive the thirty pieces of silver—his end will be the same." Suppressing his fury, Jackson then courteously attended Adams's inauguration, voted in the Senate against Clay's confirmation, and returned to Nashville, where he received a hero's welcome. Instead of just getting mad, he would get even, especially with the Judas, Henry Clay. "To him, thank god, I am in no wise responsible," Jackson wrote to a friend, "there is a purer tribunal to which in preferrence I would refer myself—to the Judgment of an enlightened patriotic & uncorrupted people." Jackson's newest war had begun. He resigned his seat in the Senate, lest anyone think that he was using the seat "for selfish consideration." In October 1825, the Tennessee legislature unanimously named Jackson its nominee for the president in 1828—the earliest such nomination by far in any presidential election to that time.[13]

Adams's disappointed presidency gave Jackson's aspirations an enormous lift. An idealistic, tortured man of great faith and great intellect, Adams hoped to use his office to improve the nation's mental and moral life, as well as its material conditions. Proclaiming a new era in which "[t]he spirit of improvement is abroad upon the earth," he wanted to mobilize the powers of the federal government to provide the people with a national university and a national observatory as well as with new roads and canals. Yet as he looked wondrously to the future, Adams also remained stuck in older, patrician ideas about politics and government as pursuits reserved for "the most able and most worthy"—educated gentlemen like himself who would guide the country to enlightened higher ground, even if at times that required overriding the wishes of their constituents. Adams despised the kinds of mass partisan politics that the Jacksonians had developed.

His Olympian style offended masses of voters who thought him a conniving, elitist mishandler of the people's money.[14]

One defeat after another plagued Adams's administration. Public response to Adams's first annual message was so negative that he suffered through what he called a "protracted agony of character and reputation," while coming to the realization that Congress would approve none of his improvement proposals. One ambitious effort, aided by Clay, to hold a major Pan-American conference that would assemble American delegates together with representatives of the newly independent nations of Latin America and the Caribbean got nowhere, undermined by pro-slavery southerners (aghast at the new republics' abolition of slavery) and by anti-administration opportunists led by Martin Van Buren. In a showdown with Georgia governor George C. Troup over the removal of Cherokee Indians from state lands, Adams at first stood firm against a fraudulent removal treaty, then backed down when Troup threatened to use military force against federal authority. Reflecting on the administration's predicaments at the beginning of 1827, Jackson's old army friend Governor Sam Houston of Tennessee observed, "[D]esperation is their only hope!!"[15]

Jackson, who had respected and even admired Adams, took special exception to the president's public spending proposals and his seemingly headstrong disregard for the electorate. "When I view the splendor & magnificence of the government" that Adams proposed, Jackson wrote, "together with the declaration that it would be criminal for the agents of our government to be palsied by the will of their constituents, I shudder for the consequence—if not checked by the voice of the people, it must end in consolidation & then in despotism." While Jackson despaired for the Republic's future, his new ally Martin Van Buren quietly assembled a national coalition on his behalf. The New Yorker had learned several lessons from the failed Crawford campaign of 1824, above all the need to unite different, even clashing interests from all sections of the country behind a single candidate. To Van Buren, Jackson was obviously the strongest alternative to Adams, and over the winter of 1826–27, he worked his magic, winning over to Jackson's cause the southern nationalist John C. Calhoun (who had settled for winning the vice presidency in 1824, and would run again in 1828) as well as various southern sectionalists—building on their common antipathy to Adams while insisting that all parties respect the sectional truce hammered out to end the Missouri crisis. Already securely based in Pennsylvania and New York, Van Buren would later add alienated Crawfordites to Jackson's ranks (including Crawford himself, a major feat), as well as anti-banking westerners (above all two Kentucky firebrands, Amos Kendall and Francis P. Blair), and even some New England patricians who had long been disaffected from the Federalist apostate Adams.[16]

Van Buren hoped that by sustaining the Missouri Compromise and suppressing national debate over volatile issues connected to slavery, he could rebuild the old Jeffersonian coalition of what he called "the planters of the South and the plain Republicans of the north," united against what he (and Jackson) considered the neo-Federalist pretensions of Adams and Clay. Once that new alliance— he called it a "party"—began falling into place in 1827, Van Buren joined with Jackson's closest political advisers (including, from Tennessee, his neighbor Major William Lewis and Senator John Eaton) to construct an electioneering machine for the coming campaign. With the Tennesseans in charge of the national headquarters in Nashville and Van Buren overseeing operations in Washington, Jackson's supporters established a string of local pro-Jackson newspapers, separate statewide pro-Jackson committees, and, down the chain of command, local Hickory Clubs to stage rallies, parades, and fund-raising events for the campaign—and to make sure Jackson voters arrived at the polls. Although Jackson himself, obeying the protocol of the day, stayed at the Hermitage and did not publicly campaign, he kept close tabs on continuing events, wrote private letters intended for publication, and made himself available to all parties interested in his candidacy.[17]

President Adams, who disdained such efforts, betrayed little confidence that he would be reelected, but Henry Clay had other ideas. Latching on to a Cincinnati scandalmonger named Charles Hammond, Clay arranged for the publication of an exposé sheet, *Truth's Advocate and Monthly Anti-Jackson Expositor*, which reported on the basis of old rumors and sheer fantasy that Jackson was an adulterer, his wife a bigamist, his mother a common prostitute, and his father a mulatto. The campaign descended into the gutter: the Jacksonians attacked Adams as a secret, decadent voluptuary and denounced Clay as an embezzler, gambler, and bordello habitué; the Adamsites responded with an ugly handbill, covered with coffins, charging Jackson with the murders of six Americans during the Creek War, as well as of Ambrister and Arbuthnot in Florida. Beneath the muck and character assassination, the respective campaigns hoped to turn the election into a contest of clashing cultural styles, between the western soldier Jackson—a barbarian, according to his foes, nature's nobleman according to his friends—and the highbrow New Englander Adams—a Christian gentleman, his own campaign said, an effete aristocrat, the Jacksonians replied.

Despite the vulgarities, however, the campaign was not simply an unprincipled and demagogic spectacle. Adams had never abandoned his moral vision of energetic government and national uplift, including his support for protective tariffs and the rest of Clay's American System, and it was on that basis that he presented himself to the voters. Jackson, drawing upon the old Jeffersonian fears of centralized power and developing an expanded trust in the virtue and political wisdom of ordinary Americans, objected fundamentally to the political ramifications of Adams's vision. Human betterment, to Jackson and his supporters, meant nothing without the support of the people. From the very start, with the "Corrupt Bargain" of 1825 (the Jacksonians claimed), the Adams presidency had been based on a gigantic political fraud; thereafter, the Adams administration had attempted to shift as much power as it could to Washington—usurpations that would more easily allow the corrupt few to oppress the virtuous many. Against Adams's formulation that "liberty is power," the Jacksonians demanded "Jackson and Reform."

Adams's early predictions of the 1828 election's outcome proved accurate. Although the contest turned out to be remarkably even in the battleground states of Ohio, Kentucky, and New York (where the voters, not the legislature, now chose electors), Jackson won them all; and he carried Pennsylvania, once again, in a landslide. In the final national tally, Jackson won 68 percent of the electoral vote and an astounding 56 percent of the popular vote, the latter figure representing a margin of victory that would go unsurpassed for the remainder of the nineteenth century. Thanks to the bitterness of the campaigns in the Middle Atlantic states, the widened practice of popular voting for presidential electors, and the organized efforts by both sides to get their supporters to the polls, those totals came from a far larger number of voters than in any previous presidential election, more than one million in all—four times the number in 1824.

Jackson's victory marked the culmination of the political unrest that had been building since 1815. A close examination of the voting returns confirms that Jackson and his managers had capitalized on the long-term fears and resentments originating in the Panic of 1819 and the Missouri crisis, and had built a popular base that combined the urban workingmen and small farmers of the North with the yeoman farmers and much of the slaveholding planter class of the South. The fractious "one-party" politics of the short-lived Era of Good Feelings had given way to a fresh political alignment. But the new politics ushered in by the election of 1828 also raised new and difficult questions. How would Jackson set about reforming the national government? How would Van Buren and the other Jacksonian managers uphold the Missouri Compromise and keep slavery issues out of national politics? Would Jackson's polyglot coalition of planters and plain republicans hold firm in the face of continuing political events? Would John C. Calhoun, now Jackson's

vice president, remain loyal? Would the defeated but hardly eliminated forces that had supported John Quincy Adams successfully
regroup, and with what new coalition of their own?

Questions also arose for Jackson himself. By defeating Adams
and winning the presidency, he had taken his continuing search for
vindication to a new level, becoming the first man of lowly birth to
occupy the presidency despite the numerous obstacles that fortune
had placed in his way. While exonerating his personal honor, he had
also, in his own mind, defeated the forces of privilege that threatened to destroy the basic principles of the American Revolution
and restore British-style, aristocratic corruption. But how would
Jackson, with so little experience in Washington, organize his new
administration? And how would a self-declared outsider sustain
that outsider's image now that he and his political advisers had
taken power?

More intimate matters also occupied Jackson's mind during the
weeks between his election and his scheduled inauguration in
March. Having long anticipated victory, he told his jubilant friends
that he felt strangely depressed when the results finally arrived. A
month later, his depression turned to anguish when his beloved
wife, Rachel—whose health, like his, had long been precarious—
collapsed and died of heart failure. The stunning blow had political
as well as personal implications. Jackson was convinced that the
Adamsites' scurrilous campaign attacks on Rachel had broken her
spirit and caused her death. And for that cruelty he laid personal
responsibility on his old foe and future nemesis Henry Clay.

# 3

# First-Term Troubles

The tumultuous inauguration of Andrew Jackson is one of the set pieces of American political lore. When the official ceremony at the Capitol concluded, thousands of spectators followed the new president to the White House, clogging Pennsylvania Avenue with their carriages and country wagons. At Jackson's insistence, the president's house had been thrown open for the day to the general public and preparations for a simple reception awaited the throngs, but the numbers proved overwhelming. Amid the melee, with well-wishers forced to climb through ground-story windows and minor damage inflicted on the official fixtures and furnishings, Jackson finally had to beat a retreat down a back stairway and return to his boardinghouse. Some observers thought the democratic spectacle sublime yet beautiful. Others agreed with Supreme Court justice Joseph Story that it appeared as if "[t]he reign of KING MOB" had commenced.[1]

Nearly forgotten is Jackson's terse and direct inaugural address. Jackson pledged to respect the sovereign powers of the states and the constitutional limitations on executive power, to sustain the military's subordination to the civil authority, and to observe "a just and liberal policy" toward the Indians. Above all, he said, the recent election had mandated that he diligently pursue "the task of *reform*," which included correcting those abuses that had placed power "in unfaithful or incompetent hands."[2]

By the end of Jackson's first term, his critics would charge that he had violated almost every one of these promises. Jackson and his supporters believed, on the contrary, that he had honored and even enlarged them. Always at stake was how Jackson defined "the task of *reform.*"

Within a month of his inauguration, the new president was busy tracking down evidence of theft and corruption by the Adams administration, with concentrated investigations in the Treasury Department. He appointed his trustworthy supporter Amos Kendall as one of the department's auditors, and Kendall immediately turned up evidence of substantial pilferage—including several thousand dollars embezzled by the last man who held his job, an ally of Clay's named Tobias Watkins. "Assure my friends," Jackson wrote to one associate in April, "we are getting on here *well*, we labour night and day, and will continue to do so, until we destroy all the rats, who have been plundering the Treasury."[3] Whether the thievery exceeded that of earlier outgoing administrations—and, if it did, by how much—is unclear. But Jackson proclaimed the scandals proved the Adams-Clay regime had been just as rotten as he had always claimed. The cure was to expand on the rotation-in-office policy he had introduced upon taking office.

Debates over rotation in office dated back to the earliest days of the Republic. During the ratification debates, anti-Federalist critics complained that the Constitution, lacking provisions for the regular automatic replacement of elected and appointed officials, would turn federal jobs into lifetime sinecures filled by abusive and insolent men. In the early months of his presidency, Thomas Jefferson enraged his Federalist adversaries by replacing numerous appointees (including several judges appointed at the last minute by his predecessor, John Adams) with Republicans. Jefferson's rotation policy was never as drastic as the Federalists charged (or as some of his more radical supporters had hoped it would be); the issue abated when the presidency remained in Virginia Republican hands through 1824, and John Quincy Adams's lofty nonpartisanship precluded a revival of the issue. Jackson, however, promised during the 1828 campaign to change all that dramatically, provoking concern among Adams-Clay men of a partisan purge of the government. With the discovery of the Treasury Department scandals, that concern turned into fears of what some called an imminent reign of terror.

The fears were exaggerated. Overall, Jackson's removals and reappointments during his presidency were roughly proportionate to Jefferson's, about one in ten. But the new president did make some sweeping changes, especially at the upper reaches of the civil service. Among government officers directly appointed by the president, the removal rate was about one-half. Land and customs officials, federal marshals and attorneys, and other high-ranking officials were subject to wholesale removal. Local postmasterships and deputy postmasterships changed hands by the hundreds. Newspaper contracts for publishing federal laws quickly fell under the control of loyal Jacksonians.

In making these replacements, Jackson had sincere reformist purposes—something his political adversaries, like many later historians, discounted. Apart from uprooting corruption, Jackson wanted to ventilate and democratize the government, especially the executive branch, by making official duties, he said, "so plain and simple that men of intelligence may readily qualify themselves for their performance." He aimed to build upon Jefferson's desire to make merit and performance, not birth and family connections, the basis for preferment. By insisting on repeated turnover of appointed executive branch officeholders—he suggested a four-year terminal limit for all jobs—he hoped to obstruct the rise of a permanent government. He also proposed limitations on the presidents who appointed them by restricting them to a single term in office of either four or six years. (Jackson further proposed eliminating the Electoral College and having presidents elected directly by the voters.) And although he restricted his idea of terminal limits to the executive branch, he hoped to democratize the rest of the government as well. He thought U.S. Senate terms should be cut from six years to four, and he would eventually envisage eliminating lifetime appointments to the federal bench and making judgeships subject to popular election.

Other Jacksonians who favored rotation had crasser motives than Jackson's. The use of government jobs as patronage for partisan loyalists had been growing at the state level since the 1790s—one reason why Jefferson, appalled by the practice, took a measured approach to rotation. By Jackson's time, political operatives in state governments approached the issue matter-of-factly, so that in 1832, when one of Martin Van Buren's right-hand men, Senator William Marcy of New York, justified the replacements and distorted Jackson's program by declaring that "to the victor belongs the spoils of the enemy," he gave the National Republican opposition a rhetorical club—"the spoils system."[4] Even before that, though, critics denounced Jackson's appointments as partisan power grabs. "Rotation" became an opposition byword for corruption—the rewarding of unsavory party hacks with government jobs.

A combination of haste and (especially on Jackson's part) gullibility lent credence to the criticisms. In making so many new appointments, Jackson came to rely on the recommendations of his political friends, which led to replacements based simply on partisan attachments. Jackson was also not always the best judge of character. Too often, he assumed that his most dependable followers shared his integrity as well as his principles. Disastrously, he made his worst appointment, an old friend and New York City fixer, Samuel Swartwout, to the collectorship of New York Port, a post with innumerable opportunities for theft. Van Buren, who was willing to go along with spoilsmanship up to a point, tried to warn Jackson about Swartwout's shady tendencies, but the president would hear nothing of it. After nearly ten years on the job, Swartwout would abscond to Europe with more than one million dollars in government funds—more than the sum stolen by all of the Adams administration's thieves combined.

The vilification of Jackson over rotation, however, was not wholly fair. By 1828, the pool of potential talent around the country had expanded well beyond the traditional criteria of worthiness. A self-made man, Jackson implemented rotation in office in order to combat insider corruption, not deepen it, or to substitute one corrupt system for another. Political thinkers with no partisan motives—including the renowned British utilitarian Jeremy Bentham—loudly applauded Jackson's policy. Some of the worst abuses of rotation, like Swartwout's, did not come to light until well after Jackson left the presidency. When Jackson did learn of misconduct—as when, early in his second term, corruption surfaced in the awarding of post office delivery contracts—he moved resolutely to end it. The great majority of Jackson's appointments performed their jobs faithfully and in some cases (such as Amos Kendall) expertly, justifying Jackson's idea about the capacities of ordinary men—including men with backgrounds like his own.

Much of the criticism directed at Jackson's appointees stemmed from an initial, contemptuous distrust of a democratized civil service. Most of the rest of it involved the taste of sour grapes in the mouths of employees who were displaced. Dejected members of the opposition had their own self-interest and amour propre, and when they eventually captured the White House in the 1840 election, they would deploy rotation just as fervently as the Jacksonians had. (This turning of the tables would one day lead a dislodged Democratic customs officer in Salem, Massachusetts, Nathaniel Hawthorne, to describe his embitterment in the opening pages of *The Scarlet Letter.*) Jackson's loftiest aspirations were compromised, sometimes by Jackson himself; reality betrayed the ideal, in this as in other areas of Jackson's presidency; eventually, the system's partisan excesses required correction, completed decades later in a series of civil service reform laws. Yet Jacksonian rotation in office introduced to Washington an important measure of democracy, with all its imperfections. To his credit, Jackson helped make the federal government more a government of and by as well as for the people.

. . .

Soon after the Treasury Department revelations, a second scandal, this one internal to the Jackson White House, hit the administration and nearly capsized it. Margaret O'Neale Timberlake, a dark-haired, vivacious beauty, was the daughter of a popular Irish-immigrant innkeeper in Washington, well known to congressmen and other government officials. Her husband, John Timberlake, a U.S. naval officer, was on active duty at sea for long periods of time, and Margaret acquired a reputation for infidelity. Especially notorious was her connection with Jackson's old friend and Tennessee neighbor Senator John Eaton, with whom she was seen in public all too often. When word arrived in 1828 that Mrs. Timberlake's husband had died at sea (a suicide, some said, depressed by Margaret's dalliances), Jackson urged Eaton to do the decent thing and marry her, and Eaton did. Jackson, paying no attention to the gossipmongers, then named Eaton as his secretary of war, to ensure that he had one close associate in the cabinet.* But a large number of the wives of official Washington, including Vice President Calhoun's imperious wife, Floride, took offense at the presence of such an obviously low woman as Mrs. Eaton in their midst and snubbed her at any social function she attended. The snubbing effectively brought social life in the White House to a halt.

Jackson immediately likened the campaign against Mrs. Eaton (known familiarly as "Peggy," warmly by her friends, snidely by her detractors) to the attacks on his late wife by the Adams campaign during the election. Ambitious men, he surmised, wanted to control him by driving his friend Eaton out of the cabinet; their supercilious wives were helping them turn social snobbery to political ends. Jackson zealously searched for evidence exculpating the Eatons

---

*The rest of Jackson's cabinet, drawn from different elements of the coalition that elected him, consisted of men he had known only briefly: Secretary of State Martin Van Buren of New York, Secretary of the Treasury Samuel Ingham of Pennsylvania, Attorney General John Berrien of Georgia, Postmaster General William T. Barry of Kentucky, and Secretary of the Navy John Branch of North Carolina.

from any wrongdoing. At one bizarre cabinet meeting devoted entirely to the mounting scandal, he thundered, "She is as chaste as a virgin!"[5]

Jackson initially fixed on Henry Clay as the manipulative genius behind the scenes, assuming that Clay was returning to his underhanded tactics of the "Corrupt Bargain" in 1824 and the campaign four years later. Then Jackson decided that the mastermind was actually his own power-hungry vice president John C. Calhoun. In fact, despite Mrs. Calhoun's prominence in shunning the Eatons, Calhoun was not the hidden instigator; and the Eaton "malaria," as it was soon called, appears to have had no clear-cut factional origins. It did, however, have immediate and important political repercussions. The cabinet wives most involved in the campaign were southerners, close friends of the Calhouns, or both, and all were long-standing fixtures in Washington salon society. The newcomers in the administration tended to side with the Eatons, and to regard her traducers as vain and ignoble. Secretary of State Martin Van Buren (a widower immune from wifely pressures) made the most of the disarray by openly soliciting the Eatons' company and doing all he could to arrange any kind of social invitation for the ostracized Peggy. Van Buren's stock with the president duly climbed as quickly as Calhoun's fell.

The furor continued for more than a year, worsening relations between Jackson and Calhoun, elevating Van Buren to become Jackson's chosen successor, and hampering orderly operations inside the executive branch. Finally, early in 1831, Jackson dismissed Calhoun's friends from the cabinet and replaced them with his own loyalists. To keep up appearances so as not to be seen as responding to a salon scandal, the president also had Van Buren and Eaton resign—although he quickly nominated the New Yorker as minister to Great Britain and arranged for Eaton's appointment as governor of Florida Territory. It was a startling shake-up, unprecedented in the new nation's history—and it placed official Washington on notice that Jackson intended to be the master of his own White House. In the aftermath of the controversy, Jackson came to depend more on the counsel of his closest political friends from outside the cabinet, including Van Buren and Amos Kendall, joined by his new attorney general, the Marylander Roger Brooke Taney— an arrangement Jackson's critics scorned as his "Kitchen Cabinet" government.

The Eaton "malaria" underscored how clashing perceptions of righteousness and sexual propriety, filtered through the parlor politics of the nation's capital, could have tremendous political consequences. Jackson, in defending Peggy Eaton so passionately, played the dual part of fatherly protector of a distressed woman and defender of the more forgiving mores of the Southwest against the vindictive uprightness of eastern high society. At bottom, the scandal described a social divide that would reappear in Washington politics down to our own time, pitting sanctimonious social and moral arbiters against new arrivals and commoners whom they deemed vulgar and uppity. Jackson took the matter so personally that he invested in it more time and energy than he should have, thereby distracting him from his reform agenda and causing him to fall prey, as he himself recognized in 1830, to "things, that have cor[r]oded my peace, and my mind, and must cease."[6] Yet as a bit of cultural politics, the drawn-out Eaton controversy offered a fresh illustration of how clashes over cultural style and morality were linked to Jackson's political rise. Later in Jackson's presidency, the clashes would contribute to the growth of a viable popular opposition to Jackson's democracy. In the short run, they intensified battles between Jackson and Calhoun over matters far weightier than Peggy Eaton's reputation.

In the late spring of 1830, while the Eaton affair was at its height, Jackson began receiving from friends incontrovertible proof that Calhoun, as secretary of war in 1818, had secretly denounced him during the fracas over his Florida expedition. When Jackson confronted his vice president and received an unsatisfactory reply, he severed all communications, calling Calhoun a Brutus in disguise.

Not only had the South Carolinian besmirched Jackson's honor in private, he had dissembled about it for more than a decade, an unpardonable act of treachery. The revelation deepened Jackson's mistaken impression that Calhoun was leading the persecution of Peggy Eaton. It also sharpened a growing division between the two men over the politics of state rights and federal power.

The conflict had been brewing for several years. In the late 1820s, pushed by a growing sentiment among political leaders in South Carolina and Georgia, Calhoun had reexamined the pronationalist ideas, similar to Henry Clay's, that had formed the core of his thinking since the start of his political career. The protective tariff became the central issue of contention. In 1824, the Congress, led by Clay and with the backing of northeastern manufacturing interests, enacted a tariff that Deep South planters deemed oppressive. Forced to sell their chief staple crop, cotton, in an unprotected world market (where prices had been steadily descending), the planters found themselves having to buy manufactured goods in a highly protected national market. They also saw the lion's share of the federal spending on internal improvements arising from tariff revenues going to the northeastern and border states. The protective tariff, they decided, was not only the source of their economic woes; it was blatantly unconstitutional, exceeding Congress's powers to raise necessary revenues and oppressing one section of the country while enriching others.

Complicated congressional bargaining led to the enactment of even higher tariff rates in the summer of 1828—in a measure dubbed by one senator as the "tariff of abominations"—and soon angry protests were breaking out in Charleston and Savannah, warning of imminent secession. Vice President Calhoun, confident he would regain his job in the autumn elections, helped stifle the rumblings with the assurance that, by working within the new Jackson administration, he and his allies could defeat the protectionists. In November, Calhoun quietly began to draft, at the request of a South Carolina legislator, a reasoned manifesto, explaining how the protective tariff was unconstitutional and outlining how individual states might fight its continued tyrannical imposition by the federal government.

The final document, approved by the state legislature in slightly diluted form and without Calhoun's signature, came to be known as the *South Carolina Exposition and Protest*. Since 1787, the *Exposition* contended, a hidden flaw in the Framers' constitutional design had emerged: a national majority, tied to a privileged sectional interest, could oppress a sectional minority with discriminatory, unconstitutional laws. The only means to ensure proper redress, in this era before the doctrine of judicial review had been fully established, was to recognize that the Constitution was a compact of completely sovereign and separate states. Should the federal government continue to oppress the minority, the *Exposition* asserted, any one state could reserve the right to revert to its original sovereignty and declare the offensive laws null and void within its borders. Should efforts to secure the abolition of those laws through constitutional amendment fail, the aggrieved state would then have the option of seceding from the Union.

Political leaders, including Jackson, strongly suspected Calhoun's authorship of the *Exposition*, which they interpreted as an effort to consolidate southern support for a later run for the presidency. But Jackson also took the idea of nullification seriously—and as a piece of rank heresy. According to his strict reading of the Constitution, Jackson held that Congress had full and direct authority over the enacting tariffs, including dictating tariff rates. To deny the rights of the majority in Congress to govern as it saw fit was, in this instance, an absurd breach of the Framers' explicit intentions. Worse, talk of nullification, let alone secession, endangered the Union. In Jackson's mind, it was an outrageous affront to the glorious embodiment of the American Revolution. "There is nothing I shudder at more than the idea of the separation of the Union," he had written to a South Carolina leader before the 1828 election. "It is the durability of the confederation upon which the general government is built, that must prolong our liberty. . . . [T]he moment it separates, it is gone."[7]

As later events would show, Calhoun's stance on nullification was actually moderate compared to what more fiery southern disunionists were thinking. Until the end of his life, Calhoun would always regard nullification as an alternative to disunion—a rational, wholly constitutional way to sustain the nation and the basic intentions of the Framers without allowing a tyranny of the majority to run roughshod over minority interests. To Jackson, however, Calhoun was engaged in sophistical hairsplitting, drawing a distinction without a difference. Nullification, Jackson insisted, was only camouflage for secession, a profanation of the Constitution as merely a compact of separate and sovereign states. Toleration of that underlying theory of state sovereignty, he charged, would lead inevitably to the nation's dissolution.

The first important confrontation over the matter occurred in April 1830, at a political banquet in honor of Thomas Jefferson's birthday, sponsored by pro–state rights congressmen from the South and the West. Knowing Calhoun would be present, Jackson arrived prepared to attack nullification, but he was not ready for the extravagant state rights sloganeering that accompanied the celebration. When his turn to deliver a toast came around, Jackson rose, glared at Calhoun, and raised his wineglass. "Our Union," he intoned, "it must be preserved." (He had meant to say "Our Federal Union," but in the excitement of the moment, he spoke more bluntly.[8]) Calhoun reportedly flinched, then delivered a wordy— some said flustered—reply, to the effect that liberty was even more important than the Union. While others in the room tried to smooth over the awkwardness, the breach between Jackson and Calhoun was now public. Shortly thereafter, and in the wake of the revelations about Calhoun's duplicity over Florida, Jackson broke off their relations.

The enmity between Jackson and Calhoun was real. For Jackson, it turned into a matter of honor, crossing into a realm where the distinction between public and private issues was murky. Henceforth, everything Calhoun now said or did would be, in Jackson's eyes, further evidence of his disloyalty. There was nothing Calhoun could do or say to redeem himself. (Calhoun, for his part, had little inclination to do so.) Jackson would be as eager for a final showdown with the South Carolinian as he had been when he called out his dueling opponents back in Tennessee.

Jackson's conflict with Calhoun was not, however, as some writers have alleged, built out of the offended president's rage at his traducer. Crucial political principles were at stake. Jackson, the democratic nationalist, truly abhorred Calhoun's view of the Constitution. Nullification, he thought, threatened the Revolution's survival. To secure the legacy of 1776, Calhoun's ideas would have to be crushed. As ever, Jackson was quick to personalize political disputes. But the clash concerned fundamentally different ideas about the nation and the national government—and in short order it would lead to a momentous constitutional crisis.

Jackson's presidency faced trouble from a disagreeable Congress as well as from divisions within the administration. In the Senate, Jackson's supporters held only a slender two-vote majority over the National Republicans; and that majority would weaken when, in 1831, the Kentucky legislature named the formidable Henry Clay to the Senate to succeed a Jackson loyalist. The administration's command of the House of Representatives, with a large majority under Speaker Andrew Stevenson of Virginia, seemed much more assured, but sectional differences undermined the Jacksonians' unity. To advance his reform agenda—and halt the National Republicans from enacting their own preferred program—Jackson would have to master quickly the intricacies of Washington power politics.

Along with rotation in office, Indian removal moved to the top of Jackson's list of priorities. The controversies over the Indians that had plagued the Adams administration heated up in 1829. Having outmaneuvered Adams over the Creeks, Georgia's governor George Troup and his successors, John Forsyth and George Rockingham

Gilmer, decided to remove the Cherokees as well, a goal made all the more pressing when gold was discovered on Cherokee land in the summer of 1829. Jackson, whose dedication to Indian removal had not wavered, sympathized with the Georgians. But he also decided it was time to impose a coherent federal policy on Indian issues, removing on a voluntary basis the remaining eastern tribes to federal lands in the territories west of the Mississippi River in exchange for their existing tribal holdings—an extension of the piecemeal allotment and relocation efforts he had overseen between 1816 and 1820. In his first annual message in December 1829, Jackson asked Congress for the funds necessary to complete his ambitious plan.

A new controversy quickly erupted, very different from the earlier one over the Creeks. With the aid of religious missionaries from New England, the Cherokees had become a model of cultural assimilation to American norms. They had shifted from hunting to settled agriculture, converted in large numbers to Christianity, adopted a written alphabet, and approved a tribal constitution based on the U.S. Constitution. These adaptations led the Cherokees to assert their sovereignty as a separate nation, which only stiffened the Georgians' resolve, and Jackson's, to see the Cherokees removed. Yet all across the country (and especially in New England) Christian humanitarians joined in a massive petition campaign demanding that Congress uphold the Indians' rights. On Capitol Hill, opposition forces, led by Senator Theodore Freylinghuysen of New Jersey, denounced the Georgians and their friends in the War Department for their frequent violations of treaties with the Indians, and charged the administration with gross materialism and callous racial prejudice. Jacksonians replied that the protests were politically motivated, engineered by partisan pseudo-philanthropists whose true motivation was to undermine the administration.

Jackson, unperturbed by his critics, played hard-knuckle politics, by making sure that the relevant congressional committees were stacked with pro-removal men and by placing pressure on wavering rank-and-file Jacksonians. The administration's removal bill passed easily enough in the Senate, along strict party lines, but resistance in the House was fierce, even among many of Jackson's nominal supporters. Pennsylvania representatives, fearing retribution from Quaker voters sympathetic to the Cherokees, were especially uneasy. Only at the very close of the congressional session in May 1829 did the House approve the bill, after protracted debate and several closely fought votes. Even then, twenty-four Jacksonians voted "nay" and twelve absented themselves. It took a solid turnout from Martin Van Buren's loyal New York delegation to carry the day for the administration. Van Buren himself, who regarded Indian removal as chiefly a southern issue and wished it had never arisen, later remarked that the outcome was so unpopular with New York voters it nearly destroyed his own political base.

Indian removal has, in recent historical writing, become the great moral stain on the Jacksonian legacy, much as it was to Christian humanitarian reformers in 1829 and 1830—a policy, supposedly, that aimed at the "infantilization" and "genocide" of the Indians, and that signaled a transition from the ethical community upheld by anti-removal men to Jackson's boundless individualism. The judgments confuse tragedy with melodrama. Compared to some of his chief political adversaries—notably Henry Clay, whose racist contempt for Indians had once prompted him to remark that their annihilation would cause "no great loss to the world"—Jackson was a sincere if unsentimental paternalist. He earnestly believed, with good reason, that his predecessors' hypocritical combination of high-minded rhetoric, treachery, and abandonment had been disastrous. Removal, he wrote, was the only practical means "to preserve this much-injured race" by placing them under federal protection, "free from the mercenary influence of White men," so that they might live as they saw fit. In view of the hard anti-Indian realities prevalent among whites in the lower South, that conclusion, although certainly patronizing to the Indians, was neither genocidal nor far-fetched.[9]

The Cherokees' demand for full tribal sovereignty was, to Jackson, unconstitutional as well as impractical. Article IV, section 3, of the Constitution stated that "no new State shall be formed or erected within the Jurisdiction of any other State" without the approval of that state's legislature. If granted, tribal sovereignty would establish an irregular nation within a nation whose existence would present as great a potential threat to national integrity and security as the Carolina doctrine of nullification. Jackson's policy owed something to his persistent fear that independent, sovereign Indian nations would prove easy prey for manipulation by hostile foreign powers. It also conformed with his developing views on the division of powers between the federal government and the states—respecting the strict integrity of the states under the Constitution, while giving the federal government considerable powers above and beyond those held solely by the state governments. In the end, quite apart from protecting the Indians, removal was, in Jackson's view, the only way to safeguard the Constitution of the United States and the nation's survival.

Yet if Jackson's removal policy was not overtly malevolent, it was insidious—and, for the Indians, it was ruinous. Jackson the paternalist presumed that all Indians were "erratic in their habits" and inferior to all whites, a prejudice then widely but not universally shared. He presumed that he understood the Indians' welfare better than they did. And, in practice, the policy never matched Jackson's own high-minded professions. Jackson's promises about voluntary and compensated relocation would be constantly undermined by delays and by sharp dealing by government negotiators that pitted one tribal faction against another to obtain land quickly and cheaply—actions that Jackson would condone. The removal bill's allotment scheme invited an influx of outside speculators, who wound up buying from those Indians who chose not to relocate between 80 and 90 percent of their land at a fraction of its actual worth. The frauds persuaded many Indians who would have preferred to stay that they had no choice but to leave. So did the sinister coercion that undergirded the entire plan: those Indians who did not relocate would be left to the tender mercies of state governments—governments whose hostility to the Indians was one of Jackson's stated reasons for favoring removal. Above all, Jackson was determined to minimize federal costs and extinguish the national debt, and provided woefully insufficient funds for the care and protection of the relocated. Although the worst suffering was inflicted after he left office, Jackson cannot escape responsibility for setting in motion a policy that uprooted tens of thousands of Choctaws, Chickasaws, and Creeks during his presidency, and that would later cost the lives of upwards of eight thousand Cherokees on the long trek west along the "Trail of Tears"—an outcome some anti-removal advocates had predicted.

The politics of Indian removal also reinforced elements within the Jackson Democracy who presumed the supremacy of whites over nonwhites, and interpreted any challenge to that supremacy as pretended philanthropy. To be sure, some of Jackson's opponents, notably Henry Clay, seized upon the issue and aided the anti-removal petition effort, contradicting their earlier views of the matter. But to reduce all of the critics, as Jackson and his supporters did, to ambitious and "factious" partisans was to confuse the opportunists with sincere humanitarians like Senator Freylinghuysen. In the political turmoil of the 1830s and after, this turn of mind would complicate and compromise the Jacksonian ideals of equality and democracy, by rendering all kinds of benevolent reform as crypto-aristocratic efforts to elevate blacks as well as Indians at the expense of ordinary white men. Those complications and compromises would, in the future, create havoc and tragedy for Jackson's party.

Congress's enactment of Indian removal, although narrowly won, was a welcome political victory for President Jackson amid the tribulations of the Eaton affair and the fracas with Vice President Calhoun. Jackson had proved that, on at least one issue, he was resourceful enough to impose his will on his faction-ridden government. He did so again, immediately after the removal bill passed, over the issue of internal improvements—this time by defying Congress instead of cajoling it.

Jackson approached federal support for road building, canal construction, and other internal improvements from a centrist posture that resembled his moderate position on the tariff. In opposition to the National Republicans who favored Clay's American System, he argued that calls for federal aid to make improvements not manifestly in the national interest were unconstitutional. Yet he would not go as far as those state rights champions, especially numerous in the South, who maligned all federal improvements; in Jackson's view, the national government had a role to play in aiding economic improvement as well as providing for the national security. Holding that middle ground inevitably led to conflict, pitting Jackson against members of his own party as well as against the National Republicans.

The divisive potential of internal improvements became apparent in March and April 1830, when Congress debated an ambitious road bill sponsored by the Pennsylvania Jacksonian Joseph Hemphill. Representative Hemphill proposed that the federal government construct a national highway running 1,500 miles from Buffalo, New York, to Washington, and then to New Orleans. The bill's backers said the road would provide a valuable military resource and a boon to national commerce and unity. To its critics, especially in the South, the bill augured an intolerable expansion of federal power that would benefit certain areas of the country more than others. In a sectional vote, the bill failed to pass the House.

More troublesome was the fight over the so-called Maysville Road bill, concerning a proposed route that would connect the town of Maysville, Kentucky, with the growing city of Lexington. Although the road would run in only a single state, its advocates claimed it would one day become an important section of a national road system and that it therefore deserved federal support. Key allies of the president, including Amos Kendall and Senator Thomas Hart Benton of Missouri, supported the measure. Southern

Jacksonians opposed it, just as fiercely as they had the Hemphill bill. This time, though, the opposition slackened, and the bill arrived on Jackson's desk for signing just as Congress was getting ready to adjourn. Jackson, certain to disappoint some portion of his coalition no matter what he did, was in a quandary. He turned to his newfound confidant Martin Van Buren for advice.

Van Buren considered himself a strict state rights Jeffersonian and he found the bill objectionable on constitutional grounds. If approved, he claimed, the Maysville bill would encourage a break-neck scramble among local interests to secure federal funds and lead to congressional logrolling. Partisan considerations also came into play, above all ensuring that the South remained loyal to the pro-Jackson alliance Van Buren had helped to forge before the 1828 election. Van Buren accordingly advised Jackson to veto the bill—an unusual step that had been undertaken only eight times by all of Jackson's predecessors. Jackson assented, and then decided to kill not just the Maysville project but a number of other improvement bills approved by Congress.

In his Maysville veto message—drafted mainly by Van Buren and by a young Tennessee congressman, James K. Polk—Jackson restated his determination, expressed in his inaugural address, to observe "a strict and faithful economy" in federal expenditures as well as "a proper respect" for the Constitution's limitations of federal power. Yet the message also emphasized that Jackson had not abandoned his previously held views about federal spending on roads and other improvements. The Maysville Road's proponents, Jackson con-tended, had failed to make their case that the project was of national and not merely statewide importance. But he reserved the power to approve any project, within "a general system of improve-ment," that met his standard of constitutionality. He would adhere to that position over the rest of his presidency, eventually releasing more than ten million dollars in federal funds for road construction, river and harbor improvements, and other ventures—a total greater than that expended on improvements by the federal government over the entire period from 1789 to 1828.[10]

The internal improvements struggle showed, as did the fight over Indian removal, Jackson attempting to carve a middle path between the reflexive antagonism to federal power exhibited by George Troup and, increasingly, John C. Calhoun, and the expansive nationalism favored by John Quincy Adams and Henry Clay. More important, it signaled Jackson's readiness to exert executive power to the utmost when his will conflicted with Congress's. To Jackson, such exertions were perfectly in keeping with his pledge at his inauguration to adhere to "the limitations as well as the extent of Executive power." To his adversaries, they would come to mark a usurpation of authority that threatened the Republic's foundations.[11]

By the end of 1831, Jackson had finally gained a grip on his troubled presidency. His break with Calhoun, and his resolve to end the Eaton imbroglio once and for all, had moved him to isolate his enemies within the administration and cut them off. His successful dealings with Congress in 1830 had cleared the way for a full reorganization of the cabinet. As part of his effort to establish control, Jackson had also arranged for the establishment of a newspaper in Washington, the *Globe*, and for the installation as its editor a Kentucky loyalist, Amos Kendall's friend Francis P. Blair. (Under Blair, Kendall remarked, the *Globe* would serve as "the friend of General Jackson and his administration, having no . . . political views other than the support of his principles."[12]) Much remained to be settled, not least the future of Jackson's national political coalition now that Calhoun and his friends were on the outs. But as a newly elected Congress assembled in December 1831 (with the Jacksonians clinging to a small majority in the Senate and still enjoying a sizable majority in the House), Jackson was ready to address the next item on his political agenda—an item he had been mulling over for some time but had addressed only briefly in public. With his new cabinet installed, he wrote to a supporter, "the great task of Democratic reform" would recommence, now as a "struggle against the rechartering of the U[nited] States Bank."[13]

# 4

## Democracy and the Monster Bank

Jackson's decision to destroy the Second Bank of the United States caught some of his own supporters by surprise. After enduring intense public opprobrium following the Panic of 1819, the Bank had recovered its reputation as a responsible financial institution thanks to the expert management of its new president, Nicholas Biddle. With its charter not due to expire until 1836, and with the "Corrupt Bargain" and the protective tariff dominating public discussion, the Bank was not an issue in the 1828 elections. Yet only a few weeks after his inauguration, Jackson was soliciting advice about how he could replace the existing Bank with a more benign institution. Near the close of his first annual message in December 1829, he cast doubt on the Bank charter's constitutionality and suggested that Biddle had failed to provide the country with a sound currency. By the late winter of 1830, Jackson's closest advisers understood his ultimate intentions. "It will come to this," Amos Kendall wrote to Francis Blair, "whoever is in favor of that Bank will be against Old Hickory."[1]

To some observers, Jackson's attack on the Bank was but the latest example of his habitual lashing out against anyone or anything he thought had insulted his honor. During the 1828 campaign, Jackson received word that Bank branches in Kentucky and Louisiana were secretly funneling funds to the Adams campaign. The charges alone were sufficient, Jackson's critics presumed, to persuade the new president that the Bank was evil and had to be destroyed. The brilliant but hardly impartial French visitor Alexis de Tocqueville picked up the claims from his numerous anti-Jackson American friends, and duly reported them as fact in his masterpiece, *Democracy in America*. The vengeful president, Tocqueville wrote, deranged by personal pique, used the full weight of his office to "rouse the local passions and the blind democratic instincts of the country" against the Bank and Nicholas Biddle.[2] Later historians unsympathetic to Jackson echoed Tocqueville's account.

Once again, Jackson's opponents misunderstood. Jackson certainly demonized the Bank and Biddle. The allegations about Bank branch interference in the 1828 campaign infuriated him. Eventually, his struggle with the Bank, like his struggle with Calhoun over nullification, became a war to defend his own reputation and honor. But, as he did with nullification, Jackson raised principled and considered objections to the Bank as an unconstitutional aberration and an affront to popular sovereignty. He believed that, contrary to the Framers' intentions, the Bank's charter concentrated extraordinary power in the hands of a small coterie of unelected private bankers—"a *few Monied Capitalists*," as he described them to one supporter.[3] Effectively responsible only to its private shareholders, the Bank amounted to an independent fourth branch of government, exercising enormous leverage over the nation's economy while operating utterly free of democratic checks and balances. No matter how expertly its president and directors performed their jobs, the Bank was, according to Jackson, inherently parasitic and aristocratic. Having sworn an oath to preserve, protect, and defend the Constitution, he thought it his duty to crush the monstrosity once and for all.

The Second Bank of the United States, headquartered in Philadelphia, was a privately owned institution with enormous public authority, of a kind unimaginable today. Under its congressional charter, the Bank served as the federal government's exclusive fiscal agent, empowered to hold government deposits, make interstate transfers of federal funds, and handle federal payments or receipts, including taxes—all in exchange for an annual fee of $1.5 million. Formally linked to the government (which owned one-fifth of its stock and appointed five of its twenty-five directors), it could use public funds interest-free for its own purposes and was exempt from taxation by the states in which it had its twenty-five branch offices. Yet the Bank was essentially a private commercial bank, beholden directly to its directors and its stockholders, an elite group numbering four thousand. Like any other chartered bank, it had the power to issue its own notes and to conduct all other normal commercial bank functions. In 1830, it was responsible for between 15 and 20 percent of all the bank lending in the country, and had issued upwards of 40 percent of all the bank notes in circulation nationwide. Its capital of $35 million was more than twice as large as the total annual expenditure of the federal government. Between 1830 and 1832, the Bank expanded further, increasing its notes and loans by 60 percent and its deposits by 40 percent. By issuing orders either to constrict or to relax its branch offices' demands on state and local banks, the Bank's president and directors could regulate lending and currency values for the entire economy.*

These were tremendous powers, and the Bank's president, Nicholas Biddle, appointed in 1823, wielded them skillfully. Under Biddle, unlike its previous presidents, the Bank was vigilant about its issuance of notes, holding a specie reserve of one-half the value of its notes issued at a time when other banks held, on average, only between one-tenth and one-quarter of their note values in specie. By keeping close tabs on financial developments around the country, Biddle transformed the Bank from a moderately profitable national branch-banking system into something more closely

---

*Essentially, the Bank operated as a debtor to the state and local banks. When state notes were paid to the federal government, the notes would be deposited in the Bank. The Bank could then regulate credit depending on how quickly it presented those notes to the state banks for payment in precious metal (or specie).

resembling a modern central bank. While it provided credit to worthy institutions and borrowers, the Bank restrained the kinds of breakneck speculation and excessive lending by state and local banks that had caused the Panic of 1819. By dampening smaller institutions' propensities to issue notes they could not back up in precious metal, Biddle helped provide American commerce with a reliable currency.

Biddle himself was an extraordinary figure. The son of a successful Philadelphia merchant and Federalist officeholder, he graduated Princeton in 1801 at age fifteen, then served in the diplomatic corps (working as James Monroe's secretary at the ministry to Britain), practiced law, edited a literary journal, and won election to both houses of the Pennsylvania legislature—all before he began his career as a banker. Described by an English visitor as "the most perfect specimen of an American gentleman I have ever seen," Biddle was no dilettante but an enormously accomplished and energetic man who seemed capable of mastering whatever vocation caught his interest. Banking was no exception.[4]

Yet if Biddle's abilities were unquestionable, the Bank's regained solidity and prominence paradoxically fed widespread misgivings about its anomalous power, and its abuses of that power, real and potential. Biddle had little regard for the mandated government involvement in the Bank's operation, minimal though that involvement was. Biddle kept the government-appointed directors on his board completely in the dark about the Bank's operations. He was contemptuous of the very idea of public oversight. Beyond the naming of its five directors, he insisted, "no officer of the Government, from the President downwards, has the least right, the least authority, the least pretense, for interference in the concerns of the bank."[5]

In these areas and others, Biddle's self-regard, combined with a certain cynicism about democracy, turned into hubris. Biddle freely distributed handsome retainers and special loans to editors and elected officials, of both parties, to ensure their support, thereby reinforcing the impression that the Bank was corrupting the government. When questioned about the Bank's powers over the nation's finances, he rashly noted that "[t]here are very few banks which might not [be] destroyed" if the Bank wanted to do so—an accurate but highly impolitic statement.[6] Biddle seemed to demand gratitude for his handling of the Bank, utterly tone-deaf to those critics who thought he ought to conduct himself and his business more as a public servant than as heaven's gift to the Republic. He also seemed to assume that his successors at the Bank (unlike his predecessors) would be just as capable as he was.

Here lay the heart of the problem for Jackson and his allies. Biddle's haughty arrogance made him, in their eyes, a living symbol of aristocratic disdain for the people and their representatives. More important, the Jacksonians believed that a bank as powerful as the Bank and an office as powerful as Biddle's—unelected and unregulated—were intolerable in a democratic republic.

Jackson's campaign against the Bank initially advanced by fits and starts. In the early months of his presidency, Jackson appears to have wanted to replace the Bank with an institution for government deposit only, without any lending or other commercial functions. Advisers including Martin Van Buren's friend James A. Hamilton (ironically, the son of Alexander Hamilton, the man behind the original Bank of the United States) affirmed Jackson's political objections to the Bank, but cautioned him against acting too drastically, pointing out the need to find some alternative to the Bank that would restrain speculation and stabilize the currency. Jackson heeded the warnings. When the distracting Eaton affair, the split with Calhoun, and the fights over Indian removal and internal improvements came to the fore, Jackson pushed the Bank issue aside until he could give it his full attention. Following the cabinet shake-up in 1831, he returned to it, vowing that "the corrupting influence of the Bank" would now be "fearlessly me[t]."[7] But by the time Jackson joined the battle, the possibility of a compromise had arisen.

The key figure in proposing a truce was Jackson's new Treasury secretary, Louis McLane. Named as part of the cabinet reshuffling, McLane was, like Jackson, a self-made man, military veteran, and lawyer who had gone on to make a career for himself in politics, in McLane's case as a congressman and later senator from Delaware. But although he was personally loyal to Jackson, McLane was also friendly with Nicholas Biddle and he approved of the Bank's role in encouraging manufacturing and privately funded internal improvements. Reinforcing James Hamilton's earlier arguments to Jackson about the Bank's benefits, McLane hammered out a compromise between Biddle and the White House, whereby Jackson would accept the rechartering of a greatly restructured Bank. McLane shrewdly couched the deal as part of a comprehensive reform of the nation's finances that would at last eliminate the national debt, another of Jackson's chief priorities. Jackson, excited by the chance that he might at last balance the government's books, consented to back off, with the stipulation that the effort to recharter the Bank not begin until after the approaching presidential election in 1832. He announced his acquiescence in his third annual message in December 1831, noting his previous objections to the Bank but handing the matter over to the Congress to do as it saw fit. The administration's intense anti-Bank rumblings seemed to have ceased.

The compromise soon collapsed, however, a victim of McLane's overreaching and factional agitation by some of Jackson's supporters. After rushing to Philadelphia to inform Biddle of the happy agreement, McLane wrote his annual secretary's report, calling forthrightly (and unwisely) for a rechartering of the Bank as well as for enactment of a protective tariff. This was too much for the sterner anti-Bank men in Jackson's Kitchen Cabinet, above all Amos Kendall and Francis Blair. Using Blair's Washington-based *Globe* as their mouthpiece, the anti-Bank Jacksonians reprinted hostile reactions to McLane's report from other newspapers and attacked what they called a recrudescence of the hated "money power." McLane threatened to resign, then worked secretly to arrange for Blair's dismissal as the *Globe*'s editor. Jackson, who had reacted calmly if a bit defensively to the criticism of McLane's report, appeared willing to stand by his secretary and the compromise with Biddle until he got wind of the plot against Blair. For Jackson, McLane's machinations amounted to insubordination that bordered on treachery. Although still formally committed to compromise, Jackson's attachment to McLane faded.

Any chance of reaching an accord died in December 1831, when 150 National Republican delegates assembled in Baltimore (in only the second presidential nominating convention in American history) and named Henry Clay as their candidate. Placing their support firmly behind Biddle and the Bank, the delegates approved an address to the nation warning that if Jackson were reelected, "it may be considered certain that the bank will be abolished." Then, quietly, Clay, along with his allies Daniel Webster of Massachusetts and George McDuffie of South Carolina, prevailed upon Biddle to seek a congressional rechartering four years early—and in advance of the election. Biddle, recalling Jackson's demand that the Bank issue be kept out of the campaign, was wary at first, but the pro-Bank politicians were persuasive. The Bank was so popular, they told Biddle, that Jackson would not dare interfere with its rechartering; and were he to try, Clay would certainly beat him in the election and get the new charter approved. Biddle, convinced that he would be better off having the inevitable face-off with Jackson sooner rather than later, went along with the plan. In January, a rechartering bill came before both houses of Congress, proposing a curtailment of some of the Bank's powers (especially in holding real estate and establishing additional Bank branches), but leaving its main lines intact.

Another contentious political issue also faced the Senate: whether to approve Jackson's selection of his new favorite, Martin Van Buren, as minister to Britain. Using the upcoming election as leverage, Clay and Webster maneuvered the vote into a tie, permitting Van Buren's archenemy Vice President Calhoun (who, as the presiding officer of the Senate, cast all tie-breaking votes) to kill Van Buren's nomination. Having humiliated the president, the

National Republicans turned to passing the Bank bill. With Pennsylvania's House members lined up solidly behind the Bank, and with New York's large delegation badly divided, the outcome was foreordained. In early July, the Bank bill passed both houses by comfortable margins. Nicholas Biddle appeared inside the Capitol after the vote to bask in the applause of his supporters, then hosted a boisterous celebration party at his lodgings that lasted well into the night, "sufficiently loud," Attorney General Roger Taney later recalled, "to make sure it would reach the ears of the President."[8]

At midnight on the evening of July 8, Martin Van Buren rushed to the White House, having just returned from his aborted ministry in England. He found the president stretched out on a chaise longue, apparently beaten down by one of his chronic ailments. Reaching up to grasp Van Buren's hand, Jackson calmly but firmly intoned a curse: "The bank, Mr. Van Buren, is trying to kill me, *but I will kill it.*"[9] Work was nearly done on a presidential message to accompany Jackson's veto of the Bank bill—a document that would spark a political firestorm.

The Bank Veto Message—drafted chiefly by Amos Kendall, but with considerable help from Taney and others, including Jackson himself—was a powerful political call to arms. Jackson and his advisers clearly designed it to reach over the heads of Congress and build public support. Discrete sections reached out to the disparate elements in Jackson's coalition, each with different reasons for opposing the Bank. For eastern workingmen and western radicals, the message contained ripsnorting polemics against the "opulent" Bank as a tyrannical monopoly. To reassure more moderate Jacksonians, it acknowledged that, although the proposed new Bank charter was unconstitutional, the Bank was in many ways "useful to the people." Southerners drawn to Calhoun would, Jackson's advisers hoped, approve the message's assertions that the bill violated "the rights of the States" and "the liberties of the People." For patriotic Americans everywhere, there were the complaints, verging on demagogy, about how foreigners, especially British investors, owned a

large portion of the Bank's stock and siphoned off American prosperity.[10]

The message offered a manifesto of Jackson's social and political
philosophy as it had developed through the first years of his presidency. Jackson's strict Jeffersonian reading of the Constitution led
him to deny the Bank charter's legitimacy on grounds similar to
those Jefferson himself had taken in opposing Hamilton's original
Bank of the United States in 1791: Congress simply lacked the
explicitly rendered powers to devise a national bank of this sort.
Jackson also indicted the proposed charter for allowing a private
institution to evade the authority of the governments of the states
in which it operated. Against claims that the Supreme Court, under
the aging Federalist Chief Justice John Marshall, had in 1819
decided, in the important case of *McCulloch v. Maryland*, that the
Bank's charter was constitutionally correct, Jackson countered that
the executive had the duty as well as the authority to uphold the
Constitution however it saw fit. In marked contrast to what has
since become the reigning doctrine of judicial supremacy, Jackson
believed that, as president, he had a responsibility to act upon his
own interpretation of the Framers regardless of the courts, and to
do so to the fullest extent permitted under the Constitution—in
this case by vetoing the Bank bill.

The message's concluding passages combined Jackson's constitutional views with his larger democratic outlook. "It is to be regret-
ted that the rich and powerful too often bend the acts of
government to their selfish purposes," Jackson proclaimed:

> Distinctions in society will always exist under every just gov-
> ernment. Equality of talents, of education, or of wealth can-
> not be produced by human institutions. In the full enjoyment
> of the gifts of Heaven and the fruits of superior industry,
> economy, and virtue, every man is equally entitled to protec-
> tion by law; but when the laws undertake to add to these nat-
> ural and just advantages artificial distinctions, to grant titles,
> gratuities, and exclusive privileges, to make the rich richer and

the potent more powerful, the humble members of society—
the farmers, mechanics, and laborers—who have neither the
time nor the means of securing like favors to themselves, have
a right to complain of the injustice of their Government.[11]

Unlike democratic liberals of later generations, Jackson abjured
using the federal government to interfere with natural "distinctions
in society," or to promote an elusive "equality" of wealth, talent, or
education. Yet in contrast to later laissez-faire conservatives, he did
not seek to curtail federal power in order to liberate business from a
corrupt, overweening government. Quite the opposite: he wanted
to liberate democratic government from the corruptions of men
and institutions of great property with political connections—the
"rich and powerful" who sought to "bend the acts of government to
their selfish purposes." In Jackson's view of America, improper
activist government meant granting special privileges to unac-
countable monied men on the make as well as to those already well
established. Sound, restrained government meant ending those
privileges and getting the wealthy off the backs of ordinary Americans, "the humble members of society." As expressed in the Bank
Veto Message, Jackson's early-nineteenth-century democratic liberalism defies today's vocabulary and categories.

The message's economic formulations were more confused. Dis-
counting Jackson's own suggestions, the authors included no con-
crete suggestions about what kind of institution might replace the
Bank—an omission that fed fears Jackson was clueless about sustaining the Bank's valuable functions. In some passages the message
lumped the Bank together with all commercial banks as "an interest
separate from that of the people," but in others it supported state
bankers' complaints that the Bank curbed too drastically their issuing of paper notes. Politics triumphed over logic and consistency: to
uphold its views of the Constitution and democracy, and to assemble
the strongest coalition possible against the Bank, the Bank Veto
Message openly contradicted itself on matters of finance and the
very banking system it was trying to end. The confusions could

stand up for only so long before Jackson would be forced to make difficult choices about how he wanted to reform the country's economy after the Bank disappeared.

Despite its combination of insight, rhetorical brilliance, and obfuscation, the veto message could not avoid alienating some portions of the Jacksonian coalition that had been forged in 1828. Old-line ex-Federalists in New England, who backed Jackson chiefly out of their abiding disgust at the Federalist apostate John Quincy Adams, were horrified. In New York City and other financial centers, where Jacksonians' opinions about Biddle were divided, committees of self-described "original Jackson men" assailed the veto while clinging to the president's name. One convert to Biddle's cause, the Manhattan editor James Watson Webb, went further, denouncing the president as a doddering old soldier who had been manipulated by "political gamblers, money changers [and] time-serving politicians."[12]

These attacks were mild compared to those launched by the National Republicans, now convinced they had pushed Jackson into a fatal corner. Daniel Webster charged that the president claimed despotic powers with the veto message, while he tried to stir up class warfare, wantonly attacking the rich "for the purposes of turning against them the prejudices and resentments of other classes." Clay asserted that an "electioneering motive" lay behind Jackson's blatant usurpation of judicial and congressional powers. In Philadelphia, Nicholas Biddle thought the message broadcast the anarchic spirit of the French Revolution, "such as Marat or Robespierre might have issued to the mob."[13] The National Republicans' revulsion was not sufficient to gain the two-thirds majorities in Congress required to overturn Jackson's veto. But now that Jackson and Biddle had turned the Bank veto into the overriding issue in the 1832 presidential election, the opposition was confident of victory. "Should Jackson veto it," Clay announced during the original debate over the Bank bill, "I will veto him!"[14] Jackson's vehemence in the Bank Veto Message solidified Clay's belief that Old Hickory had finally gone too far, and that his dangerous days in the White House would soon end.

The campaign of 1832 was enlivened by the presence of a new Anti-Masonic Party, the first approximation to a third party in the history of presidential politics. The party formed after an alleged murder in western New York in 1826 led to charges of favoritism and corruption among the Ancient Order of Free and Accepted Masons, and spread quickly in New England and portions of Ohio and Pennsylvania where large numbers of New Englanders had settled. Although churned up by populist suspicions of political insiders and hidden conspiracies, the Anti-Masonic appeal was basically anti-Jackson, pitched against the new Jacksonian politicians (notably Martin Van Buren) who appeared to have seized control of the government. Hopes arose among National Republicans in 1831 that they might ally with the Anti-Masons against their common foe in the presidential race. Those hopes evaporated when the National Republicans turned to their favorite, Henry Clay, a Grand Master Mason who denounced the Anti-Masonic crusade. Instead, the upstart Anti-Masons held the nation's first national nominating convention in Baltimore in September 1831, and selected the ex-Federalist William Wirt of Virginia, former attorney general under President Monroe, as their worthy standard bearer.

The Clay forces, after their Baltimore convention three months later, decided to attack Jackson as a corrupt would-be monarch. Over the summer of 1832, the Bank veto became the emblem of everything the National Republicans despised about the president. "The spirit of Jacksonism is JACOBINISM," one Boston newspaper exclaimed. "Its Alpha is ANARCHY and its Omega is DESPOTISM."[15] Nicholas Biddle threw his enormous resources directly into the campaign, arranging for the printing and distribution of thirty thousand copies of the Bank Veto Message—a document, Biddle believed, that offered self-evident proof of Jackson's incompetence. Only when Biddle received word that many voters actually approved of Jackson's address did he reverse course and start distributing copies of Daniel Webster's Senate speech denouncing the veto.

The Jacksonians held their own first national convention (also in Baltimore) in May 1832, chiefly to ratify Jackson's selection of Martin Van Buren as his running mate. The Jackson men then focused on the Bank issue in order to bash Clay as a sycophant of the money power. In select areas of the country—above all western New York and eastern Pennsylvania—the Bank issue played, as the National Republicans had expected, to Jackson's disadvantage. (Attacks by the Clay forces on Jackson's Indian removal policy also put the Jacksonians on the defensive in certain northern districts.) But for the most part, the Bank veto captured the voters' loyalties, with Jackson emerging an intrepid defender of the common man against privileged interests. "It is the final decision of the President," one group of supporters declared, "between the Aristocracy and the People." A North Carolinian framed the matter succinctly: "Who but General Jackson would have the courage to veto the bill rechartering the Bank of the United States, and who but General Jackson could have withstood the overwhelming influence of that corrupt Aristocracy?" Rarely has a single issue galvanized the voters in a presidential election as the Bank veto did in 1828. "The Veto issue is popular beyond my most sanguine expectations," Van Buren wrote. According to the hard-nosed, astute, and sometimes cynical Anti-Mason Thurlow Weed, the veto allowed the Jacksonians "to enlist the laboring classes against a 'monster bank' or 'moneyed aristocracy,'" thereby winning "ten electors against the bank for everyone that Mr. Webster's arguments and eloquence secured in favor of it."[16]

The presidential results were an enormous vindication for Jackson and a terrible defeat for Clay. Although the total number of voters increased by more than 100,000 over the figure in 1828, Clay actually received 35,000 fewer votes than John Quincy Adams had, a decline of nearly 7 percent. In the Electoral College tally, Jackson won 219 votes to Clay's 49 and broke the National

Republicans' hammerlock on New England by carrying Maine and New Hampshire. In their bitterness, Clay's supporters, above all Nicholas Biddle, claimed that the Bank veto had had little or nothing to do with Jackson's landslide, and that his personal popularity alone carried the day. Yet during the campaign, both Jacksonians and National Republicans sounded as if the election was a referendum on the veto, and the Jacksonians got the better of the argument. "[T]he rich—the powerful—the men who grind the faces of the poor, and rob them of their earnings," the *Vermont Patriot* declared in a typical pro-Jackson campaign piece, were attacking the president "because he will not uphold corrupt monopolies— because he will not become suppliant to the Aristocracy of the land!"[17] The themes of fraud and reform that in 1828 had focused on the "Corrupt Bargain" had now become fastened to the fight against Biddle's bank. Jackson reasonably interpreted his victory as a mandate to carry the fight forward.

The returns did not, however, lack disquieting news for the Jacksonians. In the congressional races, the pro-administration side ran poorly, reducing its House majority by thirteen seats compared to four years earlier. More ominously, in the Senate, the slim Jacksonian majority disappeared completely: at the next session, the opposition would hold a majority of eight. Compounding the problem was the Anti-Masons' strong turnout in the northeastern states, enough to give William Wirt 8 percent of the overall popular vote for president. Should the Anti-Masons and the National Republicans ever find a way to unite, the alliance could cause Jackson men enormous trouble in the North.

Of even greater immediate concern, though, were the results in the South, especially in John C. Calhoun's South Carolina. Outside Maryland and Clay's home state of Kentucky, the Jacksonians swept through the slaveholding states, much as they had in 1828. But in South Carolina, forces friendly to Calhoun in the state legislature (which still named the state's presidential electors) delivered the state's seven electoral votes to a breakaway state rights candidate,

Governor John Floyd of Virginia. In seven other southern states, dissenters ran a ticket with Jackson at its head but with the pro-Calhoun Virginian Philip Barbour substituted for Martin Van Buren. These little schisms did not affect the election's outcome. But they did have enormous implications that would lead, in the weeks immediately after the election, to a showdown even fiercer than the one caused by Jackson's veto of the Second Bank of the United States.

5

---

# The Nullifiers' Uprising

While Jackson staked his presidency on the Bank veto, he tried to eliminate the protective tariff as an important campaign issue. His own view on the tariff had shifted. Once a moderate protectionist, Jackson had decided that the protectionists and anti-tariff men alike had greatly exaggerated the tariff's effects on national prosperity and growth. And in any event, reductions in federal spending were easing the government's reliance on tariff revenues. In 1832, the White House duly backed a downward revision of the abnormally high rates of the extant "tariff of abominations," cutting those rates, on average, by half. The proposal preserved a mild protectionism while bowing to southern demands for dramatic cuts—sufficient, the president hoped, to quiet the nullifiers and their theorist, John C. Calhoun, without offending his northern Jacksonians in pro-tariff states like Pennsylvania. Jackson appeared to have prevailed when, in July, the administration bill passed both houses of Congress by comfortable margins, gaining the support of a large majority of representatives from the slaveholding states in the House and a respectable southern minority in the Senate. But to South Carolinians, who staunchly opposed any tariff aimed at protection, the bill was an outrage that caused many to abandon all lingering faith in the federal government. Less than a month after Jackson had secured his reelection, a specially elected convention in Columbia declared the new tariff null and void inside the sovereign state of

South Carolina and vowed to secede from the Union should Jackson try to enforce the nullified law.

Tensions over state rights had led to talk of disunion since the Republic's early years. In the political emergency that followed the enactment of the alien and sedition laws in 1798, Jefferson and Madison had drafted their Kentucky and Virginia Resolutions, hoping to galvanize the state governments to interpose between the citizenry and a tyrannical Federalist government. New England Federalists' protests over President Jefferson's embargo and then the War of 1812 had culminated in the Hartford Convention and the region's flirtation with secession and making its own peace with the British in 1814. None of these failed precursors augured well for South Carolina's bid for nullification in 1832. But the state's protests were tied to slaveholders' fears over slavery's future as well as over federal policies. The distressed South Carolinians believed, not unreasonably, that antislavery sentiment was abroad in the world, threatening what they considered their orderly, respectful, and Christian regime. The fight over the tariff was part of the planters' larger struggle for self-preservation, and they engaged in it furiously. The South Carolinians also had before them a full treatise, the *Exposition and Protest* of 1828, which justified nullification and explained how it should proceed.

The semi-anonymous author of that treatise, Vice President Calhoun, would take a restrained position during the nullification crisis, standing up publicly for his doctrines but at the same time urging moderation among the nullifiers and remaining open to compromise. For President Jackson, however, nullification in any form was treason, and the movement had to be completely destroyed. And to Jackson, the root causes of the uprising were the dishonorable ambitions and philosophical claptrap of John C. Calhoun and his supporters.

Anticipating the worst, South Carolina's most determined nullifiers, led by Governor James Hamilton, Jr., and Congressman George McDuffie, set to work mounting a resistance movement well before the revised tariff was enacted. Having already formed a States' Rights and Free Trade Association, they redoubled their efforts (with Hamilton the chief organizer) over the winter of 1831–32, founding a new political party and holding two separate conventions, in Columbia and Charleston, that warned of dire consequences if Congress did not dismantle the protective tariff. There was, however, significant opposition to the nullifiers within South Carolina, from old-line Federalist conservatives who prized the ties of Union and rejected nullification as a radical innovation, as well as from up-country yeomen in the hilly northern counties (called "parishes") who had long been suspicious of the low-country planters' power. Confident that these Unionists were the stronger force and that his new tariff proposal would defuse discontent, President Jackson seemed unworried. "You may expect to hear from So Carolina a great noise . . ." he wrote to his old friend John Coffee in July, "but the good sense of the people will put it down."[1] Events would prove Jackson was utterly mistaken.

In the years since Calhoun drafted the *Exposition and Protest* southern fears over slavery's future had been intensifying. The rise of the cotton kingdom after 1800 had given southern slavery a new lease on life—but did so just at the point when northern states were embracing antislavery and completing the gradual emancipation of their own far smaller numbers of slaves. The debates between 1819 and 1821 over Missouri's admission to the Union raised the fearsome specter of disunion, hardening both the northern antislavery view and the southern contention that slavery was a benevolent, even sacred institution. Then the discovery in 1822, in Charleston, of what appeared to local officials to be a conspiracy among free blacks and slaves following the leadership of an ex-slave carpenter, Denmark Vesey, raised alarms all across the South that northern antislavery talk might incite bloody slave insurrection.

Events during the early years of Jackson's presidency further convinced slaveholders that their property and their way of life were besieged. Anxiety mounted in 1829 and 1830, when officials in Charleston and other southern seaports intercepted copies of an incendiary pamphlet—written by a Boston-based free black, David Walker, and smuggled south—bidding the slaves to overthrow their masters. A few months later Walker suddenly died, in what looked to some like suspicious circumstances. A short time after that, a white Bostonian, William Lloyd Garrison, established a new radical newspaper, *The Liberator*, dedicated to bringing about slavery's immediate demise. Just as ominously, antislavery advocates in the Virginia legislature forced a debate over a gradual emancipation plan early in 1832. Although the proposal failed, that the Virginians even discussed abandoning slavery shocked slaveholders in the Deep South, and especially in South Carolina. (Virginia, one disgusted South Carolinian remarked, had become "infested" with "Yankee influence.") Threatened from without and within, slavery's defenders began to see any effort by the federal government to enact policies they deemed unfavorable to the South as part of a larger antislavery design. This included the protective tariff, which one state rights' party convention in South Carolina declared was intended to hasten "the abolition of slavery throughout the southern states."[2]

That South Carolina took the lead over slavery and the tariff is not surprising. Along with Georgia, the state had long produced the most articulate and outspoken champions of slavery. (By comparison, leaders from the border slaveholding states, notably Henry Clay of Kentucky, expressed more ambivalence about slavery's alleged benevolence.) In no Deep South state did the slaveholders enjoy a more thorough command over political, social, and cultural life. Lacking an extensive up-country of yeoman farmers, South Carolina's planters were spared the kinds of democratic challenges that roiled politics elsewhere in the region. Old-line low-country families and newer cotton-boom entrepreneurs from the interior forged a remarkably united elite that honored what its members regarded as valuable traditions—"the old things," William Grayson, the Beaufort-born poet and congressman remarked, such as "old books, old friends, old and fixed relations between employer and employed."[3] South Carolina also contained the South's largest proportion of slaves relative to its total population, making its white population especially touchy about abolitionist agitation and possible slave rebellions. The Vesey affair, and then the appearance in Charleston of Walker's pamphlet, had concentrated wonderfully the minds of white South Carolinians.

John C. Calhoun, the theorist of nullification, was the most powerful political leader in the state, and he fully shared in the apprehensions about the North's ultimate intentions regarding slavery. Slaveholders, he wrote one close friend in 1830, might "in the end be forced to rebel, or submit."[4] Yet unlike Hamilton, McDuffie, and the more radical nullifiers, Calhoun, even after his break with Jackson, did not think the time was ripe for drastic action. The South would do better, he believed, to unite under his command, displace Jackson, then build a national majority that would defeat Yankee despotism without taking the steps of interposition and nullification. Precipitate action—"in every way imprudent," he observed—could ruin those plans by isolating South Carolina from the more moderate southern states. Yet throughout 1830 and 1831, Calhoun could see more radical sentiments building in his home state. Finally, under pressure from Governor Hamilton, he decided to write an open letter for publication from his plantation, Fort Hill, that, without endorsing those he privately called "the Carolina hotspurs," defended nullification as a fully constitutional check on northern tyranny. For the first time, Calhoun publicly declared his attachment to the nullification idea. Rather than be left behind, he now joined the nullifier campaign in order to help give it direction as well as energy.[5]

Nullifiers finally squared off against Unionists in the 1832 campaign for the state legislature. The fight was especially tense in the northernmost portions of the state as well as in Charleston (where local artisans along with old-line Federalists rejected the nullifiers, and where mobs from the opposing sides clashed in the streets). The nullifiers won 61 percent of the total vote, though, thanks to lopsided margins in the rural slaveholding districts, and under the state's malapportioned system of representation, the nullifiers gained the two-thirds majority in the legislature that, under the terms laid out by the *Exposition and Protest*, was required to call a special nullification convention. Called into special session by Governor Hamilton, the new legislature quickly approved the new convention, to be elected without delay. The Unionists, disappointed and divided, put up a minimal fight for convention seats. In full command of the convention's proceedings, the nullifier delegates approved, in late November, an ordinance of nullification, which would come into effect on February 1, 1833.

Jackson, forewarned by the South Carolina Unionist Joel Poinsett, had already taken precautions against the nullifiers, including ordering the federal forts in Charleston harbor to prepare for attacks and sending revenue cutters to the waters off the South Carolina coast to collect the tariff before merchant ships came close to shore. Several days after the nullification convention passed its ordinance, he delivered his annual message and included a proposal that looked like an effort at conciliation, even appeasement: expeditiously lowering the tariff to cover only what was necessary for federal revenue and national defense, provided that all sides in the dispute exercised "moderation and good sense."[6] Although the message rejected what Jackson took to be the nullifiers' disunionist folly, the president seemed willing to accede to the South Carolinians' basic demand. But the message was deceptive. Having come to view the tariff rate levels as of marginal importance, Jackson was not sacrificing his policies or principles. Further, in calling for calm and reason, Jackson was setting himself up as the wise and flexible man in contrast to the South Carolina hotspurs. With soothing words, he would reinforce his old connections with southern officials and isolate the nullifiers. That done, however, he would then show the nullifiers no mercy—as he proved, only six days after the annual message, by releasing a special proclamation on December 10, 1832, that he hoped would destroy nullification forever.

The differences between the message and the proclamation have confused historians much as they did many of Jackson's opponents.

("One short week produced the message and the proclamation," a baffled Henry Clay wrote to a political ally, "the former ultra, on the side of State rights—and the latter ultra, on the side of Consolidation. How can they be reconciled?")[7] Some have argued that Secretary of State Edward Livingston, who drafted the proclamation, was its true author, thereby portraying Jackson as a captive of his diverse cabinet with no consistent beliefs of his own. Others blame an outburst of Jackson's hatred of John C. Calhoun for the proclamation's violent rhetoric. Kinder critics fault Jackson for contradicting himself in the second document, as part of a failed attempt to compensate for the apparent mildness of the first.

These interpretations are based on false presumptions, and they explain too much. Having Livingston draft the proclamation was perfectly in keeping with how Jackson's White House operated, as it was with the way presidents, before and since, have composed important statements.* Jackson habitually turned to cabinet members and other advisers to write his important state papers, sometimes relying on his more nationalist allies, sometimes on more state rights–oriented men. Always, however, he was in charge, overseeing the process of composition, freely contributing his own ideas and prose, and allowing nothing to go out under his name that did not reflect his own thinking exactly. The nullification proclamation was no exception; indeed, Jackson probably worked harder and more directly on the proclamation than on any other official statement of his entire presidency.[8] (Not only did he help write certain vital passages and endorse the final product; he sharply rebuked

---

*Alexander Hamilton, for example, was the coauthor of President George Washington's famous Farewell Address in 1796, and James Madison offered advice as well. In the modern era, the greatest addresses of Franklin Roosevelt, John F. Kennedy, and Ronald Reagan were largely written by speechwriters and aides, often, in Roosevelt's case, following protracted consultation with interested parties in which the president participated. Even Abraham Lincoln, perhaps the finest and most assured writer ever to serve as president, had advisers review his speeches from time to time. Yet in all cases, final credit, correctly, has gone to the presidents themselves—Jackson being a major exception.

those in his coterie, including Blair and Kendall, who later attempted to mute the proclamation's stark language.) Nor can Jackson's loathing of Calhoun explain his loathing of nullification, built as it was on the nationalist principles he had held long before he broke with the vice president.

The fundamental misperception behind these erroneous interpretations is that the two documents actually conflicted. The common view is that Jackson, by taking a "low tariff" position in the message, was loudly endorsing southern state rights, whereas by blasting nullification, he was endorsing a nationalist—indeed, "ultranationalist"—reading of the Constitution. But Jackson saw the issues of the tariff and nullification as completely separate. According to Jackson's strict reading of the Constitution, the tariff, subject to approval by the Congress, was always negotiable. Depending on which side could muster majorities in the House and Senate, tariff rates might rise one year and fall in another, in line with the normal pull and tug of a representative democracy. Nullification, however, was not negotiable; rather, it was an assault on the very foundations of the Union and democratic government. In the nullification proclamation, Jackson dissected the difference.

Jackson began by knocking down each of the South Carolinians' constitutional arguments about the tariff. To the nullifiers' claim that high tariff rates stemmed from an unconstitutional desire to protect manufacturing and not merely collect necessary revenues, Jackson replied that there was no such thing as unconstitutional motives, only unconstitutional acts. The nullifiers charged that the tariff operated unequally on different regions; Jackson pointed out that a perfect equality in any system of taxation was impossible and that, in any event, this hard fact offered no justification for states to nullify legislation over which the Framers had explicitly given Congress jurisdiction. The tariff, said the nullifiers, raised monies later appropriated to internal improvements projects that even Jackson deemed constitutionally dubious. But that objection, Jackson observed, was irrelevant to the point at issue, the tariff itself.

Jackson then took aim at the heart of the matter, the nullifiers' theory of the Union and undivided state sovereignty, as enunciated by Calhoun. These inventions, Jackson declared, were patently absurd, produced by "[m]etaphysical subtlety, in pursuit of an impractical theory." The nation had not been created by a compact of sovereign states; in fact, the nation was older than both the Constitution *and* the states. Prior to independence, "we were known in our aggregate character as the *United Colonies of America*"; under the original Articles of Confederation, the states were subservient to the Congress in areas delegated to Congress; when framed and ratified "to form a more perfect union," the Constitution became a new charter for an already existing nation. "The Constitution of the United States . . . forms a *government*, not a league," Jackson concluded. With no preexisting undivided state sovereignty to fall back on, nullification was utterly illogical as well as illegitimate. Any state's denial of the federal government's designated powers was a denial of the Constitution that would lead, inevitably, to the Union's dissolution—and thus, in Jackson's view, to the failure of the American Revolution and its experiment in popular sovereignty.[9]

Above all, Jackson's nullification proclamation, far from a defense of "consolidation" or "ultranationalism," arose from Jackson's belief in democracy and in the principle, as he had expressed it in his first annual message, *"that the majority is to govern."* Strict construction of federal power was imperative lest a minority (like the owners, directors, and supporters of the Second Bank of the United States) bend the government toward advancing the minority's interests. But no state—let alone "a bare majority of voters in any one state"—could be allowed to repudiate laws based on explicitly delegated powers and duly enacted by Congress and the president.[10]

Some of Jackson's strongest and most prominent backers—to say nothing of the South Carolinians and their southern sympathizers—could not comprehend his reasoning, and saw the proclamation as unnecessarily harsh and at variance with old Jeffersonian principles. Ordinary Jacksonians were not so bewildered or offended.

Over the early winter of 1832–33, most of the legislatures in the non-slaveholding states (as well as Maryland) passed resolutions condemning nullification and affirming Jackson's hard-line stance. In cities from New York to New Orleans, large public meetings acclaimed the president. In mountainous, yeoman-dominated eastern Tennessee, one old Jackson comrade, John Wyly, contended that Old Hickory would be able, inside of two weeks, to raise enough troops to mass them at the state border and "piss enough . . . to float the whole nullifying crew of South Carolina into the Atlantic."[11]

The southern slaveholder-dominated legislatures were more divided. The Georgia and Virginia legislatures contained powerful minorities that favored nullification. North Carolina lawmakers condemned nullification as lawless and subversive, but refused to support Jackson's proclamation. Alabama called for a federal convention to take up the crisis. And Jackson's belligerence deepened many southerners' sympathies with South Carolina, as a lonely state facing a possible armed assault by federal troops. Yet though Jackson rattled his southern constituency, no southern state came to the nullifiers' support. In his firmness, Jackson had forced the issue of nullification's legality—and outside South Carolina, no state, even in the Deep South, was willing to contest him on that.

Jackson, seemingly unaffected by the proclamation's critics, pushed on with his military preparations—determined to enforce the law however he could, and to ensure that, if the crisis should turn violent, the nullifiers would be the ones to fire the first shot. One week after the proclamation, he ordered Secretary of War Lewis Cass to ascertain how quickly men and munitions could be mobilized sufficient to "crush the monster in its cradle." In South Carolina, Governor Hamilton resigned on December 13 to head the state's newly enlarged armed forces, and the legislature then selected Calhoun's friend the moderate nullifier Senator Robert Hayne as governor. The legislature also named Calhoun, who had resigned his lame-duck vice presidency effective December 28, to succeed Hayne in the Senate, then handed the state's presidential electoral votes to Governor Floyd of Virginia. With the rhetoric escalating and soldiers drilling for combat, it appeared as if the federal government and South Carolina—and Jackson and Calhoun—were headed for their great showdown. But Jackson's proclamation proved, in retrospect, a turning point. South Carolina was politically cut off—and very quietly, moderating influences began asserting themselves in Washington and Columbia.

The crisis played itself out over the first two months of 1833. Governor Hayne, trying to avoid an overly aggressive posture, ordered that the 25,000 volunteers who had rallied to the nullifiers' cause train in their hometowns rather than gather at Charleston. Jackson, lowering his voice, asked Congress for specific powers to raise federal troops and state militias summarily should the South Carolinians forcibly seize federal property. In its content as well as its tone, Jackson's message was firm and measured, but the nullifiers ripped into it as a tyrant's provocation and labeled Jackson's request for military support as the Force Bill. Calhoun, now back in the Senate, led the assault on Capitol Hill, calling Jackson's request an imperial edict. Yet Calhoun, though confrontational in public, was playing his part behind the scenes to reach an accord with Clay and Webster, and to defuse the situation in Columbia. Calhoun would not stand down from Jackson, but he wanted to resolve the crisis peacefully.

At the end of January, with the South Carolina nullification ordinance due to take effect in one week, the state, in a tactical retreat, agreed to postpone the implementation until Congress had resolved the tariff issue. Calhoun pressed the more radical nullifier leaders to keep calm and avoid even considering secession "but in the last extremity." He also urged Hayne and others to suspend the nullification ordinance for a year. Virginia sent a commissioner to Columbia to deliver copies of the legislature's resolutions that criticized both nullification and Jackson, and offered to mediate the dispute. The White House forwarded a new low-tariff bill to Congress, sponsored by one of Van Buren's New York allies, as the basis for a compromise.

Neither Calhoun nor the National Republicans wanted to have anything to do with the administration's latest tariff bill. They were convinced its enactment would look like a victory for their common enemy, President Jackson. So Calhoun, Clay, and Webster began hammering out their own compromise bill. Clay and Webster, insistent that northern protectionists would go no further than a gradual adjustment of tariff rates, got the better of the bargaining, and forced Calhoun to back down on every important point. The final draft of the compromise called for a small reduction of the 1832 rates, then a very gradual decline in tariff duties until 1842, when the rates would drop sharply to the levels sought by the nullifiers. To spite Jackson, Calhoun ended up agreeing to a bill that brought a measure of relief to angry southerners, but that amounted to considerably less than the end of supposedly unconstitutional protection—and less than Jackson had seemed to offer in his annual message in December 1832.

The Force Bill issue remained, and on this both Calhoun and Jackson were determined to make a stand. This time, however, Calhoun had to battle against northern National Republicans as well as Jackson, while Clay and his moderate border-state allies repaired to the sidelines. The highlight of the Force Bill struggle saw Calhoun pitted against Webster, in debates that drew packed crowds to the Senate gallery. But by the time the speeches ended, Congress's approval of the Force Bill was all but assured, due to Jacksonian control of the House and the divisions between nullifiers and southern moderates in the Senate. And so, in somewhat clouded circumstances, the nullifiers quietly cut a deal whereby they would forswear their efforts to block the bill's passage and Congress would assent to the compromise tariff. When both measures passed, Calhoun took the Senate floor and delivered one last eloquent (and irrelevant) denunciation of the Force Bill. Thereafter, he left Washington directly for Columbia, to make sure that the more radical nullifiers would see the light and acquiesce.

There was little chance that the South Carolinians would persist. As soon as Congress passed the compromise tariff, the main issue had been resolved, and what support the nullifiers had received from other parts of the South disappeared. The nullification convention duly reconvened and, on March 11, rescinded its ordinance. As a largely symbolic parting shot, the delegates approved a new ordinance that nullified the Force Bill. They had lost on almost everything of practical importance, but they would not surrender their honor.

"I have had a laborious task here," Jackson wrote to one of his cousins in the spring, "but nullification is dead; and its actors and exciters will only be remembered by the people to be execrated for their wicked designs." The president, having vindicated his own honor as well as the Union's, overestimated his victory. In the South, even staunch Jacksonians admitted that, although nullification was impermissible, Jackson had overreacted and defended ideas that endangered state rights. "You can rest assured," one anti-nullification, normally pro-Jackson Mississippian told a friend, "S.C. has our sympathies." Many northern Jacksonians, although far more supportive of the president, still found his words and actions disquieting—at odds with Jeffersonian orthodoxy and unnecessarily antagonistic. Martin Van Buren, for one—concerned as ever about keeping the Jacksonian coalition intact and now anticipating his own eventual run for the presidency—could not get the New York legislature to unite in support of Jackson's nullification proclamation, and he personally opposed the Force Bill. Other anti-nullifiers saw the outcome as ominous in the long run. "Nullification has done its work," the South Carolina Unionist James Petigru wrote. "It has prepared the minds of men for a separation of the states— and when the question is moved again it will be distinctly union or disunion."[12]

Still, Jackson had good reason to feel victorious. With a mixture of angry threats and well-timed moderation, he had isolated the nullifiers and suppressed the immediate threat before him, without firing a single shot. Compared to his predecessor Adams's handling of challenges to federal authority, Jackson had acted with fortitude and cunning. Although he got no credit for the compromise tariff that was eventually enacted, he outmaneuvered the nullifiers, pushing Calhoun into a position from which he ended up negotiating away supposedly nonnegotiable demands. Of all the major parties to the controversy, only Jackson had sought to lower the tariff and pass the Force Bill—and he got his way on both measures.

There was, to be sure, a great deal more to the nullification crisis than was fully apparent in the public accusations and debates. As Calhoun suggested early on, the struggle arose from the growing alienation of southern slaveholders, whose "peculiar domestick institution" placed them in "opposite relation to the rest of the Union." As James Petigru understood, the Compromise of 1833 did not settle the underlying issues of slavery and Union any more than the Missouri Compromise had. Jackson and his supporters could not see these deeper causes, and instead blamed the crisis on Calhoun's and the nullifiers' personal ambitions, either to dislodge Jackson or to break up the Union and install themselves as potentates. The impulse behind nullification, the Jacksonian *Globe* asserted, was "a *politician's*, not a *planter's*."[13]

If he misunderstood all that was at stake, though, Jackson presented a powerful and, for the moment, triumphant case about the central issue, the legitimacy of nullification. He thereby showed (contrary to the claims of many later historians) that protection of the democratic Republic, and not the protection of slavery, was his animating political principle. Devotion to the nation, the Constitution, and the will of the majority, Jackson declared, took precedence over allegiances to region, state, and locality. In defending that belief as he did, Jackson offended some of his own supporters, especially in the South, yet still squelched the nullifiers' uprising. He also established a crucial political and constitutional precedent.

In later decades, southern slaveholders, expanding beyond Calhoun's arguments, would push the idea of state rights in protection of slavery to the point of disunionism. In 1861, they would force a secession crisis, once again centered on Charleston harbor, far more severe than the confrontation over the tariff in 1832–33. And when that happened, Jackson's successor Abraham Lincoln would rely on Jackson's nullification proclamation and his uncompromising actions for political guidance and strategic lessons.

Less than two days after Congress passed the compromise that ended the nullification crisis, Jackson was sworn in for his second term as president. He could look back with great satisfaction on what he had accomplished thus far, especially during the previous twelve months: gaining personal command of his administration, securing his Indian removal bill, vetoing the charter of the Second Bank of the United States, thwarting nullification, replacing John C. Calhoun with his chosen favorite, Martin Van Buren—and, in his reelection campaign, crushing Henry Clay. Along the way, he had aroused the support of some constituencies and lost that of others, building and refining what would soon emerge as a coherent national party, the Democracy.

Yet Jackson still had powerful adversaries to face, and important issues to resolve. Despite his victory in the presidential campaign, Jackson would now have to deal with a Senate firmly in the control of the National Republicans—and led by the ever-resilient Henry Clay. The struggle with the Bank of the United States, with four years left to run on its charter, had hardly been settled. Although nullification had failed, neither the southern fears nor the northern antislavery agitation that inflamed them would cease simply because of the successful enactment of a tariff. "General Jackson," wrote John Quincy Adams's son Charles Francis, shortly after the second inaugural, "conquers every thing."[14] But the conqueror could not rest on his past successes amid the unruly commotions of his second term.

# 6

## The Second Battle of the Bank

Near the end of the 1832 campaign, Jackson began to contemplate commencing a new assault on the Second Bank of the United States, to finish the job he had started with his veto of the Bank charter. The Bank's support of Jackson's adversaries was more overt in the 1832 election than it had been four years earlier. Nicholas Biddle appeared willing to spend the Bank's funds freely in order to get his way. And neither the veto nor Jackson's electoral victory guaranteed Biddle and the Bank's defeat. With four years still left to him at the Bank, Biddle could manipulate the financial system and cause a crisis. Voters, the Jacksonians feared, would blame them for the collapse and elect opposition candidates to the White House and Congress, who could reverse Jackson's veto and recharter Biddle's bank. "The hydra of corruption is only *scotched not dead*," Jackson wrote in December to the young Tennessee congressman James K. Polk; Biddle's political friends, he was certain, intended to "destroy the vote of the people lately given at the ballot boxes" and restore the monster.[1]

Jackson's prediction that Biddle would fight brutally to the finish proved sound. Yet by launching a preemptive strike on the Bank, Jackson also complied exactly with his opponents' image of him as a reckless and vengeful autocrat. The resulting political war dominated Jackson's second term and sharpened the country's polarization over financial and economic issues. Jackson would win another costly victory and divide his party yet again. National politics turned at last into a contest between two coherent parties, Jackson's Democracy and the reformed opposition, which called itself the Whigs. In time, Democrats and Whigs would battle over many issues, from banks and currency reform to the constitutional limits on executive power. But they were galvanized, initially, by their views of one man, Andrew Jackson.

Jackson faced serious opposition from within his own party, and even his Kitchen Cabinet, over expanding the attack on the Bank. Van Buren, as ever, was squeamish. The Jacksonian-dominated House rejected a bill, sponsored by Polk, that declared the federal deposits in the Bank unsafe and called for their removal. When the disappointed president proposed summarily withdrawing the government deposits on his own, his adviser James Hamilton called the idea "questionable" and repeated his warnings that swift and dramatic action might cause a "great disturbance in commercial affairs." Amos Kendall was the outstanding exception among Jackson's counselors, goading the president to head off what he envisaged as Biddle's inevitable counterattack against the veto, and to reassure his supporters that he would finish the job he had started. Over the summer of 1833, while consulting with the editor of the *Globe*, Francis Blair, and Attorney General Roger Taney (who also backed withdrawing the deposits), Jackson dispatched Kendall to seek out suitable state-chartered banks as possible recipients of government funds. He also tried to win over his more fearful allies. "[I]s it possible that your friends hesitate, and are overawed by the power of the Bank?" he asked Vice President Van Buren with a gentle touch of mockery. "[I]t cannot overaw[e] me. I trust in my God and the virtue of the people."[2]

The opposition's later charge that Jackson had partisan motives in withdrawing and dispersing the government's Bank deposits contained a kernel of truth: as Kendall wrote, transferring the funds to sympathetic state banks would "raise up powerful friends" to the administration. But the enrichment of loyal state banks, whom the opposition derided as the "pets," was more an effect than a cause of

Jackson's war on the Bank. Distributing federal monies to state banks was not an innovation: President Madison had followed the same necessary course in 1811 after Congress refused to recharter the original Bank. Perceiving Biddle and his friends as unconstitutional connivers—a "corrupt league," Kendall called them—Jackson was not about to place the withdrawn funds into banks loyal to the Bank. The main purpose behind Jackson's latest move against the Bank was the same as it had always been, to rid the nation of an establishment, he wrote, that threatened "the perpetuity of our republican institutions" by allowing an "aristocracy" of "the wealthy and professional classes" unchecked power over "the mass of the people." The pets would prosper as a result—but would do so by performing legitimate functions, with proper oversight by the Treasury Department, and not as the mere recipients of partisan patronage.[3]

The summer of 1833 brought another major reshuffling of the cabinet. Secretary of State Edward Livingston had long desired a reposting as minister to France, which Jackson approved, then named Treasury Secretary Louis McLane (with McLane's full assent) as Livingston's successor. McLane recommended as the new Treasury secretary the lawyer William John Duane of Philadelphia—a longtime advocate of banking reform and critic of the Bank, the son of Jackson's old friend and ally William Duane, but also a man who had worked closely with Philadelphia's formidable Girard family bank, a firm with national influence that had long been a rival of the city's old Federalist establishment. Jackson took McLane's advice, then presented the cabinet with an outline (drafted by himself and Roger Taney) for commencing removal of the Bank deposits on October 1. All that was required to begin was the new Treasury secretary's formal approval. But Duane, surprisingly, balked, claiming that on the Bank issue he was more beholden to Congress than to the president. Enraged, Jackson proceeded anyway. On September 20, the *Globe* announced Jackson's plan. Five days later, Jackson fired Duane and named Taney as his replacement.

Although still subject to Senate approval, Taney was now in charge of overseeing the deposit removals. He proceeded cautiously. On the one hand, he understood that withdrawing the funds too rapidly would have an unsettling and perhaps devastating effect on the entire economy, not just on the Bank. On the other, he was certain that Biddle would try to foil Jackson by retaliating against the selected pet banks as best he could. To ward off Biddle, Taney gave five of the seven pets a total of $2.3 million in Treasury drafts on the federal deposits in the Bank. Should the Bank crack down on any of the pets by presenting them with notes and demanding specie payment, the pets could fire back with the Treasury drafts, withdraw additional funds from the Bank, and preserve their own liquidity. But Taney's plan backfired. Three days after the removal order went into effect, but before Biddle made any major public moves, one of the state banks Taney had tried to protect presented drafts worth $100,000 to the Bank, in order to cover an unsuccessful stock speculation by one of the bank's directors. Biddle now had the pretext he needed to commence a drastic contraction of the Bank's credit. By January 1834, following additional withdrawals by the state banks, Biddle had reduced the Bank's credit load by $9 million.

Biddle had been planning to strike since he first learned of Jackson's intentions to withdraw the deposits. As early as July, he warned the Bank's New York branch of his plans to "crush the Kitchen Cabinet." On the day the removal order went into effect, Biddle enlisted his directors to agree to eventual contractions of credit. In private, Biddle admitted that he hoped to cause general distress and force the House to abandon its party allegiances and join with the Senate in coming to the Bank's aid. No matter what, he would save his beloved bank. "My course is decided," he blustered to one friendly congressman, "all the other Banks and all the merchants may break, but the Bank of the United States shall not break." Taney's ill-fated Treasury draft scheme gave Biddle temporary political cover from charges he was purposely causing financial havoc to frustrate President Jackson.[4]

Biddle's contraction had the economic effects he desired, touching off business failures and causing unemployment to rise to levels that some feared would surpass those that followed the Panic of 1819. One New York Democrat observed that in Manhattan the suffering was "as great as any community can bear." Biddle's friends and supporters immediately blamed the disaster on the irresponsible autocrat Jackson and what the patrician New Yorker Philip Hone called his "supererogatory act of tyranny." Worse, for the Jacksonians, complaints arose inside their own ranks. "[M]any of [Jackson's] partisans are in much distress," one New Hampshire senator wrote, "under the impression that his lawless and reckless conduct and his obstinacy will prostrate the party."[5]

Jackson did not flinch. When groups of businessmen came to the White House begging him to change course, the president brushed them off sternly. "Go to Nicholas Biddle," he roared at one delegation from New York. "We have no money here, gentlemen. Biddle has all the money. He has millions of specie in his vaults, at this moment, lying idle, and yet you come to *me* to save you from breaking. I tell you, gentlemen, it's all politics." Jackson was playing a shrewd psychological game, deploying his well-known fury to convince the world that he would risk everything, including the nation's prosperity, before he gave in to Biddle and the Monster Bank. (Once the New York businessmen had headed down the White House staircase, the president was heard to chortle, "Didn't I manage them well?") The ploy convinced some notables that the banking crisis had turned into fateful civil war. "The present contest," Edward Everett of Boston remarked to an English banker, "is nothing less than a war of Numbers against Property."[6]

The Bank War made some strange political bedfellows. In the Senate, Henry Clay led the National Republican attack on Jackson's Bank War—and was joined by Senator John C. Calhoun. The ironies of Calhoun's position were manifold. Having played a major role in creating the Bank in 1816, Calhoun had since moved away from his nationalism and become a fearsome critic of Clay's American

System—yet now he was back, allied with Clay, standing not so much as a defender of the Bank but once again as a nullifier foe of Jackson and (he claimed) Jackson's continued usurpation of power. Together, Clay, Calhoun, and their respective followers, joined by congressional Democrats offended by the removal of the deposits (soon branded as Conservatives), tried to obstruct the president at every turn. Jacksonian solidarity in the House remained strong enough to pass a series of resolutions, required by the Bank's charter, accepting a report from Taney that declared Biddle's contraction had rendered the government deposits unsafe. But the Senate not only rejected Taney's report, Clay sponsored a censure resolution against Jackson condemning the firing of Duane and the removal of the deposits as unconstitutional actions, "dangerous to the liberties of the people."[7] For three months, the resolution lay open before the Senate, allowing Jackson's enemies to denounce the president repeatedly. Finally, their point made, Jackson's foes approved Clay's resolution.

Jackson responded to this latest blow with a strong and lengthy formal reply, drafted chiefly by Van Buren's former law partner, Benjamin F. Butler, whom Jackson had appointed as attorney general to succeed Taney. Claiming, erroneously, that the executive branch had exclusive control over handling federal revenues, the message required a quick clarification and partial withdrawal. Otherwise, it was a powerful presentation of Jackson's views regarding the Constitution, politics, and presidential power. Jackson argued, not unreasonably, that the Senate had bypassed the Framers' measured procedures for impeachment by censuring him. He had been stained with charges of what amounted to high crimes and misdemeanors against the Constitution without the right to defend his actions in a trial by the House. Clay knew that he lacked the votes in the House to impeach Jackson and instead had appealed to the Senate to harass the president; it was strictly politics in the Bank War. But from Jackson's perspective, the Senate's censure established a dangerous precedent by twisting the Constitution for partisan gain and by making the Senate appear superior to the executive.

Jackson's reply also elaborated his larger ideas about a democratic presidency. On the question of William John Duane's dismissal, Jackson charged that the Constitution only gave the Senate the power to advise and consent over nominations to executive posts. Once approved, cabinet officers served solely at the pleasure of the president. The president, moreover, had a special position in the federal government, along with the vice president, as "the direct representative of the people." Clay's censure resolution tried to undermine that constitutional distinction by granting Congress, "a body not directly amenable to the people," a power over the executive branch neither stated nor envisaged by the Framers. Clay and others had accused Jackson of usurpation; on the contrary, Jackson retorted, it was his opponents who wished to usurp the president's authority by inventing new congressional privileges in order to oversee and bully the executive. If Clay's censure stood, the federal government would move closer to resembling a parliamentary system, directly contradicting the intentions of Madison and the other Framers.[8]

None of this impressed the Clay-Calhoun coalition. The Senate approved the censure a second time by a larger margin than before, and did not even allow Jackson's protest to be included in the Senate journal. Outside Washington, however, the tide was turning against Nicholas Biddle and the Bank, the actual sources of all the trouble. Infuriated by the Bank's continued contraction of credit, business leaders from New York and Boston demanded over the spring and summer of 1834 that Biddle relent lest they repudiate him publicly and bring fully to light how his policies were harming the nation. Finally, in mid-September, Biddle gave way, resuming the Bank's lending, halting the so-called Biddle Panic, and ending his effort to force Jackson's hand.

The downturn's economic effects turned out to be less severe than expected, thanks in part to the state banks' emissions of paper currency, which sustained the nation's overall money supply. But the Biddle Panic, and the Bank War generally, brought dramatic and lasting political changes. Prior to 1833, Jackson's policies had caused various elements of his original political coalition to defect. Yet these offended constituencies had little basis on which to unite with each other or with the National Republicans. Calhoun and the southern nullifiers were basically at odds with constitutional nationalists like Clay and Daniel Webster, as well as with ex-Jacksonians whose main complaint was the Bank veto. The protective tariff and Clay's American System were anathema to erstwhile pro-Jackson slaveholders. The surprisingly popular northern Anti-Masons, although ill disposed to Jackson, remained alienated from Henry Clay, a Mason.

The continuation of the Bank War provided these groups, as well as Conservative Democrats opposed to the deposit removals, with a rallying point—not in support of the Bank (which, as even Clay began to realize late in 1834, was beyond salvation) but against Jackson as an executive tyrant. To National Republicans and Conservative Democrats, Jackson was a would-be Caesar, whose power rested on the support he and his minions had whipped up from the frenzied mob. To Christian humanitarians, Jackson was a despot who tolerated human slavery and force-marched the Indians to the West. Nullifiers and their southern sympathizers considered Jackson a traitor to state rights. Anti-Masons saw him as an arrogant insider who had built a corrupt partisan organization and then had set himself above the law—and who, like Clay, was a Mason, but with incalculably greater power.

These shared antipathies also derived from the Jacksonians' own growing confidence and capacities as a political party, now known simply as the Democracy. After winning the White House with their polyglot coalition of 1828, Jackson and his lieutenants had refined their party's policies and reinforced their organization. From the top of political society to the town, village, and ward levels, Jackson supporters had constructed a coherent new national political structure, focused on electing other Jackson supporters to office. State and local party conclaves would select candidates and enlist loyalists to get out the vote. Party newspapers, from the *Globe* in the nation's capital down to sheets turned out in rural printing offices, spread the Democracy's message, kept politics roiling between elections, and advertised the activities of the local Hickory Clubs and other pro-Jackson associations. In the Bank War and the nullification crisis, the Jacksonians also hammered out a political ideology and identity far sharper than the amorphous "reform" program of 1828—an ideology that combined three interwoven strands: robust nationalism on constitutional issues tempered by a restraint on federal support for economic development and a strict construction; a distrust of what Jackson called the corrupting power of "associated wealth"; and a celebration of what one pro-Jackson newspaper called "[t]he democratic theory . . . that the people's voice is the supreme law."[9]

The anti-Jackson opposition attacked this democratic talk as claptrap, broadcast by men whose primary allegiance was not to the people or the Constitution but to the disgraceful elevation of Andrew Jackson. By the spring of 1834, energized and unified by their assaults against Jackson, the enlarged opposition had discovered a name for itself, adapted from the nation's revolutionary lore—the Whig Party, befitting the political and spiritual descendants of the Whig patriots who had battled King George III. Under "[t]he happy cognomen of Whigs," one North Carolina newspaper exclaimed, "all parties opposed to Executive usurpation" could now "rally in defense of LIBERTY against POWER."[10]

It would take a great deal more thought and energy for these new Whigs to build a national political organization and hone a distinct ideology to match the Democracy's. Declaiming against power and in favor of liberty seemed, on its face, at odds with what had long been the National Republicans' expansionist and nationalist argument that, as John Quincy Adams put it, "liberty *is* power." It was not enough for the Whigs to declare that Jacksonians' partisan organization was inherently corrupt. To construct their own party and to mobilize their own supporters at election time, they would need more than anti-Jackson zeal. Above all, the Democracy projected the forward-looking optimism of men breaking down old or revived privilege, opening the way for ordinary American citizens to claim their share of liberty and prosperity. It was utterly impossible to defeat the Jacksonians, the former Anti-Mason and now fledgling Whig from New York William Henry Seward observed in 1835, so long as they appeared to embody the very principle of democracy, posed as a conflict of the poor against the rich. "[S]ince the last election," Seward lamented, "the array of parties has strongly taken that character."[11]

By the time Seward offered his gloomy assessment, the Bank War had entered a new and furious phase. Its outcome would further polarize the parties over banking, finance, and the battle between rich and poor—with ironic and eventually painful consequences for the Jackson Democrats.

On January 30, 1835, as President Jackson departed a ceremony at the Capitol, a madman lunged from the shadows, pointed a pistol at the president's chest, and squeezed the trigger—the first presidential assassination attempt in American history. The gun misfired, then misfired again; Jackson, unafraid, brandished his walking stick like a club and tried to beat his assailant to a pulp, before onlookers interceded and had the gunman arrested. Judged insane, the would-be assassin, an unemployed British immigrant housepainter, was locked away in an asylum. Jackson concluded that Providence had spared him from a dark conspiracy laid by one of his many political opponents. Others, like the pro-Jackson New York *Evening Post*, judged the incident "a sign of the times," provoked by the intense passions stirred up by Jackson's leadership.[12]

For Jackson, the times brought a mixture of disappointment and encouraging news. In 1834, the Senate, while censuring him, had also rejected his nomination of Roger Taney as secretary of the Treasury. In the House, dissident Democrats had helped elect the opposition candidate, John Bell of Tennessee, as Speaker, defeating Jackson's loyalist James K. Polk, while Whig congressmen blocked a bill that would have provided federal regulation of the removed deposits. Yet the House also approved resolutions in favor of the deposit removals, and the administration won passage of a Coinage

Act, intended to substitute gold coins known as "Jackson eagles" or "Benton gold lozenges" (in honor of the hard-money Jacksonian Thomas Hart Benton) for bank paper in everyday business transactions. Most auspicious of all for Jackson, the Treasury Department had announced that, thanks to continued receipts from the tariff and Jackson's insistence on applying them to debt reduction, the federal debt, which stood at more than $58 million when Jackson took office, would be completely extinguished as of January 1, 1835. In an editorial coinciding with the anniversary of the Battle of New Orleans, the *Globe* cheered Old Hickory's two great victories, "the first of which paid off our scores to *our enemies*, whilst the latter paid off the last cent to *our friends*."[13]

The erasure of the debt eventually turned out to be a political curse in disguise. By the end of 1835, the federal surplus reached an astonishing $17 million; debates over what to do with the funds complicated Jackson's efforts to prepare for the death of the Bank's charter the following year. Those efforts had proceeded apace since the end of Biddle's panic. Although formally committed to giving his pet bank experiment a full and fair chance to prove itself, the president intimated that he was willing to support the establishment of a new "Third" Bank of the United States, publicly directed and headquartered in Washington, which, above all, would help shift the nation to a metallic currency for most transactions. The plans for a new bank got nowhere, but Jackson's efforts to alter the nation's currency, in line with so-called hard-money banking principles, became the core of his final reform efforts.

Hard-money champions had a long lineage in American politics. In the 1790s there were critics of the Hamiltonian banking and paper money system; the Panic of 1819 rekindled hard-money believers, as did the writings of various eastern labor radicals and western opponents of Clay's American System. But hard-money ideas finally crystallized as an economic doctrine in the aftermath of Jackson's Bank veto, particularly in the writings of the Philadelphia journalist and bank critic William Gouge. In a cogent, massively documented treatise published in 1833, *A Short History of*

*Banking and Paper Money in the United States,* Gouge argued that only a metallic currency could spare the nation from wrenching boom-and-bust economic cycles and protect the government from corrupt private bankers. Picked up by Jackson's admirers (including Francis Blair), Gouge's *History* became something of a sensation. Early in 1835, the new Treasury secretary Levi Woodbury (appointed and approved in lieu of Taney) hired Gouge as a department adviser; for many years thereafter, Gouge and his supporters would be the chief architects of Democratic banking and money policy.

The hard-money argument was at once economic and political—but it was not, contrary to many accounts of Jacksonian policy, dogmatically laissez-faire. Banks, hard-money reformers asserted, tended to overissue their paper notes, leading to speculation and inflation. When, as a consequence, the value of paper money fell, causing a drain on bank supplies of precious metals, the banks were forced suddenly to cut back on credit and bank-note issues, which inevitably led to financial panic and economic disaster. In the aftermath, a few fortunate speculators bought up the property of the ruined at cut-rate prices—and the accursed cycle began anew. Only the removal of paper as the basis of exchange in ordinary business transactions could prevent the insecurity and chronic hard times (or, as the *Globe* put it, "the casualties and frauds") inherent to the speculative paper system.[14]

Banks, under the existing system, also corrupted American democracy, the hard-money men insisted. Limited to the commercial sphere, bank lending of paper to large borrowers was legitimate and worthy—a commercial function that did not impinge on the functions of the federal government. But to give commercial banks control over the value of the currency was a plain violation of the Constitution, granting "too great a power," Benton wrote, "to be trusted to any banking company whatsoever." It was up to the government to reassert its sovereignty by ending the banks' control and reasserting its own constitutional responsibilities to oversee the currency. The Whigs, bridling at what they considered this gross interference, would call these hard-money proposals a call to "war

on the currency of the country . . . on the merchants and mercantile interests" in order "to support the power of the federal government."[15]

Jackson regarded hard-money principles as perfectly in line with
his own thoughts about banking and currency, and his move toward
adopting strict hard-money policies accelerated after intense speculation and inflation resumed late in 1834. Several factors contributed to the latest overheated boom. Jackson's dispersal of the
federal deposits to the pet banks, by removing the supervision once
provided by the Bank, encouraged irresponsible bank lending. But
Secretary Woodbury curbed these abuses by making federal
deposits in a pet bank contingent on the bank's restraining its note
issues—thereby turning the Treasury Department, he later
explained, into something approximating a regulating "central
Banking institution."[16] More significant were the effects of the burgeoning federal surplus, a fortuitous glut in silver caused by inter-
national bullion flows, and a speculative frenzy in the buying of
federal land in the western territories in late 1834 and 1835. As the
federal government continued to accept paper money for land purchases, that flow of paper westward turned into a flood, filling the
Treasury's vaults with worthless currency. And without formal suppression of the circulation of small-value notes nationwide, currency values dropped even more, despite the ameliorative effects of
the Coinage Act.

The administration proceeded with steady incremental reforms,
trying to perform the services formerly performed by the Bank
while hastening the transition to a hard-money currency. In February 1835, Congressman Polk introduced to the House a bill, earlier
rejected by the Senate, that would have banned American receivers
from accepting any bank's notes valued at less than five dollars,
while also requiring all federal deposit banks to hold in specie one-
quarter the value of the notes they had in circulation. The proposal
got nowhere, but Woodbury later ordered the deposit banks not to
issue notes worth less than five dollars or to accept such notes in

payment of debts owed the government. A year after that, Congress prohibited issuing notes under twenty dollars, effective March 1837, and approved a provision requiring the convertibility of all paper notes into specie on demand.

The banks' unconcerned continuation of the boom hampered the administration's efforts, as did obstructionist moves in Congress. Biddle's Bank, still an important factor in the credit market, shifted from contraction to runaway expansion late in 1834, increasing its loans by $15 million during the first six months of 1835. Smaller banks followed suit, and the amount of paper money in circulation rose nearly one-third by year's end to $108 million. Benton, speaking in the Senate, worried that the hard-money reforms would not come into effect quickly enough before history repeated itself: "The revulsion will come," he predicted, "as surely as it did in 1819–'20."[17]

The Whigs fought Jackson's reforms by reviving an old proposal of Henry Clay's on land sales. Jacksonians, including Benton, had long advocated cheap-land policies, holding the purchase costs of federal land to a minimum in order to help ordinary settlers stake their claims out west. Clay and his followers, more interested in development than in mere settlement, had called instead for a system that emphasized distributing a portion of land-sale receipts directly to the states. The plan would circumvent Jackson's strict constructionist objections over providing federal aid to purely local internal projects by giving money to the state governments, who would then use it for local projects—a roundabout method of expanding federal aid for road building and other improvements.

Pushed aside during Jackson's first term, the idea stirred renewed interest when the federal debt was retired in 1835, and attention focused on the new and burgeoning government surplus. In a revised proposal, Clay offered 15 percent of the total revenue from federal land sales to the states and territories in which the sales occurred, with the rest set aside for general distribution to the remaining states. Soon after, Calhoun proposed a bill for regulating the federal deposit banks, which the Senate Banking Committee, controlled by Whigs and Conservative Democrats, then knit together with Clay's distribution plan. The resulting legislation, called the Deposit Bill, increased regulation of the state banks and curtailed further small-note issues, but opened the way for a surplus distribution scheme that the Jacksonians deemed unconstitutional—and, they feared, would worsen rampant speculation by handing funds to the states to do with whatever they wished. The bill also increased the number of deposit banks to eighty-one with the not so subtle aim of enlarging the portion of pets friendly to the Whigs—a move that, by dramatically increasing the sheer number of banks, would also severely hamper Secretary Woodbury's efforts to oversee and rein in the banking system.

Certain that the Whigs were deliberately engineering another financial crisis, Jackson privately threatened to veto the Deposit Bill when Congress passed it in June 1836. In the end, he decided against it. He was fearful that depositing the new federal surplus directly into the existing pet banks would be perceived by the voters as patronage politics, a potential sore point in the looming presidential election. With the Deposit Bill in place, the speculative land bubble, as forecast by Benton and others, swelled to new heights. The federal land office, meanwhile, had turned into an enormous government-sponsored land racket, whereby speculators bought large parcels of federal land with paper money, then used the land as collateral for additional loans.

In July, after Congress had finally adjourned, Jackson, now in the final year of his presidency, had Woodbury issue what came to be known as the Specie Circular, requiring gold or silver payments for the purchase of all federal land. The circular had an immediate impact, destroying the speculation in government land and rendering completely worthless millions of dollars in paper money. Congress reconvened for a brief session in December and outraged Whigs and Conservative Democrats rammed through a bill rescinding the circular and restoring paper-money purchases of government land. Jackson quietly killed the bill with a pocket veto.

. . .

By bursting the speculative bubble, the Specie Circular delivered a shock to the economy that many writers, then and now, would blame for the disastrous financial panic that began scant months after Jackson left office. The blame is one-sided. The circular, although certainly drastic and costly, did not halt land sales as thoroughly as is often assumed. Purchases continued, but in metallic currency, which required large transfers of specie from the East over the winter of 1836–37. More important, the Treasury Department had earlier transferred specie westward, in anticipation of the Whig-Calhounite Deposit Act's debut, stripping eastern banks, especially New York City banks, of the vast majority of their specie reserves. By early 1837, the banks were extremely vulnerable to any external forces—including British demands for specie payments from American debtors—that added to the strain. The Jacksonians' hard-money reforms, put into place to forestall a crisis, came into existence too late. In fact, the Deposit Act, whose impact the Specie Circular was designed, in part, to overcome, helped wreck the economy as much as the circular itself.

Jackson realized that his opponents had frustrated his hard-money experiment and understood that the economy had fallen into precisely the kind of artificial speculative boom he had hoped to quell. He blamed the irresponsible state banks as well as the Whigs and Conservative Democrats, and cast about for a fresh policy. In the weeks following the announcement of the Specie Circular, he again considered proposing a revised plan for a constitutionally correct "Third" Bank. But by then Jackson's presidency was nearly over, the race to elect his successor was well under way, and there was little point in forwarding a proposal that could easily boomerang against the Democrats as a betrayal of their anti-Bank faith. Jackson kept his own counsel. The inflationary boom continued. The revulsion that Thomas Hart Benton had predicted would finally occur in May 1837.

In time, the Whigs took full political advantage of the perceived utter failure of Jackson's banking and currency policies—and Jackson would pay a dear price among later historians. But in 1835 and 1836, the boom stifled complaints from the public at large about the administration's handling of the economy, while the effects of the Biddle Panic hurt the opposition. In the 1835 state and congressional elections, the last major political test before the presidential election, the Whigs fared poorly, especially in northeastern areas where they expected to run well. "All looks fearfully, hopelessly black," the Anti-Mason turned Whig Thurlow Weed remarked, upon receiving news of the Jacksonians' sweeping statewide victories in, of all places, Connecticut, until then one of the most reliably anti-Jacksonian states in the Union.[18]

Had financial and economic issues alone stirred the electorate, Jackson's chosen successor, Martin Van Buren, might have looked forward to an easy victory in 1836. But other issues had come to the fore since 1832, with dire implications for Van Buren or any other Democratic presidential candidate from a northern state. The most taxing—and, potentially, the most costly—surrounded the growing northern abolitionist movement and the difficulties the Jacksonians faced in keeping debates over slavery out of national politics.

# 7

---

# Slavery and Democracy

Andrew Jackson was one of the most successful cotton planters and slaveholders in Tennessee. He came of age just as the questioning of human bondage by liberal, Enlightenment-influenced planters was fading. In the newly born cotton kingdom, Jackson bought, sold, and owned black slaves as a matter of course. Unlike his political hero Thomas Jefferson, he appears never to have doubted the morality of slavery (although, like Jefferson, he condemned the transatlantic "traffic in the poor african," outlawed in 1808, as "illegal and inhuman"). As president, he regarded the rising antislavery movement as a political threat to the nation and the Democracy, and he disparaged abolitionist campaigns as veiled efforts to instigate slave rebellions. Radical abolitionists disparaged him in return as a fiend who, as William Lloyd Garrison of Boston wrote, deserved to be "manacled with the chains he has forged for others and smarting under the application of his own whips."[1]

It is easy to judge Jackson according to neo-abolitionist standards, to condemn him as slaveholder and, even further, as pro-slavery. Such verdicts, though, too often have more do with the self-regarding sanctimony of posterity than they do with history; and in Jackson's case, they obscure far more than they illuminate. The president's primary political objective lay not in promoting slavery but in abiding by the spirit of the Missouri Compromise and keeping the divisive slavery issue out of national politics. The abolitionists represented, after 1830, a small minority of northerners in Jackson's time, and an even smaller minority of northern whites, and Jackson considered them a noisome and perilous distraction from the fight to save democracy and the Constitution from "the money power." A fierce anti-abolitionist, Jackson also attacked those pro-slavery southerners, preeminently the South Carolina nullifiers, whom he believed endangered the Union in order to advance their personal and sectional interests. If he never questioned slavery, neither did he endorse the view, shared increasingly in the 1830s by slaveholders generally, that the institution was a positive good ordained by God.

Jackson approached the slavery issue primarily as a political question, not an ethical one. On that account, his presidency today looks callous, to the point of appearing, in one scholar's description, *"functionally* pro-slavery." Yet many of Jackson's slaveholding contemporaries considered him and his party highly suspicious on slavery issues—insufficiently militant in suppressing the abolitionists, overly harsh in suppressing nullification, and more interested in securing national political power than in protecting slaveholders' rights. And after 1835, a small but growing number of northern Jacksonians extended the Democracy's egalitarian principles to the politics of slavery, denouncing the Jackson administration's efforts to quash the abolitionists as crude violations of free speech, and portraying what one Ohio Jacksonian famously called "the slave power" as no less a threat to democracy than the Bank of the United States and the money power.[2]

Ultimately, the stance taken by Jackson and mainstream Jacksonians on slavery was tragic. Pointing to the protections afforded slavery by the Constitution, Jackson and his devotees rebuffed abolitionists like Garrison who proclaimed slavery a national sin that required immediate eradication (and who, in time, would call the Constitution a pact made in hell). Sensitive to southern fears of slave revolts, and wrongly persuaded that wealthy and privileged northerners were provoking antislavery agitation in order to disrupt the Democracy, the Jacksonians struggled to placate the slaveholders' ire without capitulating to the pro-slavery political ambitions they associated with John C. Calhoun. Yet in trying to insulate politics from the slavery question, Jackson and his party only antagonized the most determined antislavery and pro-slavery factions. In trying to lay to rest debates over slavery, and protect their egalitarian, democratic ideals from being engulfed by sectional controversy, they aroused troublesome disputes over the very meaning of equality and democracy—disputes that in 1860 would sunder both the Democracy and the Union.

Like others of his political generation, Jackson forged his views on slavery and national politics in the crucible of the Missouri crisis of 1819–21. Enraged by slavery's continued geographic expansion, northern Jeffersonian Republicans, in alliance with some surviving Federalists, attempted to block Missouri's admission to the Union as a slave state. Their arguments renounced slavery as an immoral departure from the Declaration of Independence's credo that all men are created equal, and insisted that Congress had the power to determine the status of slavery in new states. Pro-slavery Republicans replied angrily that slavery was not a curse but a blessing, and that any interference by Congress with slavery in Missouri would be a gross attack on state rights and the Constitution. Finally, forces of compromise manufactured their testy truce, whereby Missouri would be open to slavery (further infuriating the antislavery northerners), but that slavery would be banned in states and territories obtained in the Louisiana Purchase that lay north of latitude 36° 30' (further upsetting the pro-slavery southerners).

Virtually every important political figure of the decades to come—Henry Clay, John Quincy Adams, Martin Van Buren, John C. Calhoun, Nicholas Biddle—either had a direct hand in completing the Missouri Compromise or endorsed it, with varying degrees of enthusiasm. Andrew Jackson, though living at the Hermitage, without a military commission or political office, was no exception. His initial reaction to the controversy, which he shared with men as diverse as Clay, Calhoun, and the aging Thomas Jefferson, was to blame a Federalist political conspiracy for even raising the Missouri matter.

Federalism had been floundering since the War of 1812, seemingly on its last legs, reduced to a small sectional party concentrated in portions of New England and New York. Because the old Federalist stalwart Rufus King (late of Massachusetts, now of New York) had delivered some of the most eloquent speeches on the antislavery side, many, including Jackson, surmised that the true motive behind the agitation was to revive disgraced Federalism as a powerful northern party. The slavery issue, according to this view, was only a pretext, seized upon by Anglophilic aristocrats in hopes of reversing, at last, the triumph of Jeffersonian democracy. In stirring up that prickly issue, the congressional Federalists—denounced by Jefferson as "Hartford convention men"—thought nothing of endangering the Union itself.[3]

Jackson, Jefferson, and the others were mistaken about the factional political origins of the crisis. The main instigators were neither Federalists nor crypto-Federalists but Republicans from all across the North, who were sincerely troubled by slavery's expansion and who denounced slavery, in (ironically) Jeffersonian terms, as an affront to human equality. But the instinctual fear that any serious engagement over the slavery issue presaged national disunion was sound. Jefferson famously wrote of hearing "a firebell in the night" amid the Missouri debates, which he at once considered "the knell of the Union." John Quincy Adams observed that the crisis "disclosed a secret," that the North could be united over halting slavery's spread. "[H]ere was a new party ready formed . . . terrible to the whole Union, but portentously terrible to the South— threatening in its progress the emancipation of all their slaves."[4]

Jackson, as a slaveholder, resented the northern interference and thought it provocative and unconstitutional, but worried chiefly about what it portended for the Union. In a letter to his ward Andrew Jackson Donelson, he explained his thinking:

> The Missouri question so called, has agitated the public mind, and what I sincerely regret & never expected, but what now I see, will be the entering wedge to separate the union, it is

even more wicked, it will excite those who is the subject of discussion to insinuation and masacre. it is a question of political asscendency, and power, and the Eastern interest are determined to succeed regardless of the consequences, th[e] constitution or our national happiness. they will find the southern & western states equally resolved to support their constitutional rights—& I hope I may not live to see the evills that must grow out of this wicked design of Demagogues, who talk about humanity, but whose sole object is self aggrandisement regardless of the happiness of the nation.[5]

For the rest of his life, Jackson would see the politics of slavery and antislavery as a virtual reprise of the Missouri crisis, incited by self-interested troublemakers, a threat to slaveholders' constitutional rights, liable to arouse slave rebellions, but above all "a question of political asscendency, and power" that left unchecked would destroy the Union.

The political bargaining that ended the Missouri crisis raised powerful hopes that men of good will had achieved a final adjudication of the slavery issue. Although southerners complained about the 36° 30' provision, Jackson's friend and neighbor Senator John Eaton wrote that "they ought not, for it has preserved peace, dissipated angry feelings, & dispelled appearances which seemed dark & horrible & threat[en]ing to the interest & harmony of the nation." Secretary of War John C. Calhoun, another pro-compromiser and, in 1820, still Jackson's friend, noted that although the crisis had somewhat weakened southern and western slaveholders' attachment to the Union, the failed agitators had "destroyed to a great extent their capacity for future mischief." Jackson would follow them, standing by the Missouri Compromise as a pillar of his party and his presidency.[6]

Respect for the compromise was essential to Martin Van Buren's strategy to build a pro-Jackson coalition of the "planters of the South and the plain Republicans of the north" in the 1828 election.

Assembling that alliance required gaining the support of men who had held diverse views on the Missouri question, from antislavery northerners who had vowed never again to help elect a southern president to the more refractory southerners who viewed the compromise as a sellout of the South's constitutional rights. Among the latter was the influential editor Thomas Ritchie of Richmond, Virginia. In a famous, cajoling letter to Ritchie, written early in 1827, Van Buren spoke of the need to build a new party that would halt the northern "clamour agt. Southern Influence and African Slavery." Historians who see Jackson and the Jacksonians as essentially proslavery have offered these statements as decisive proof of their claims.[7]

Yet Van Buren, who had played a large role in securing the Missouri Compromise, was speaking not *as* a pro-slavery man but *to* a pro-slavery man, whose support for Jackson he badly wanted. While he understandably emphasized to Ritchie how northern "clamour" was the source of the crisis over slavery (which in the case of Missouri was perfectly accurate), he was bidding the Virginian, much as he bid antislavery northerners, to drop their hotter sectional views and back a candidate, and a fledgling party, dedicated to preserving the compromise and thereby the Union. Van Buren's ultimate purpose, like Jackson's, was to defeat what he saw as the resurgent neo-Federalism and corruption of the Adams-Clay regime, and restore what Jackson later called "good old jeffersonian Democratic republican principles."[8] By that reckoning, any political agitation over slavery, whether by the North or the South, was a priori an effort to obstruct the advance of democratic republican principles.

President Jackson and his advisers watched with anxiety as northern antislavery opinion took a more radical turn early in Jackson's first term, first among blacks such as the pamphleteer David Walker and then by radical whites like the "abolition now" proponent Garrison. Those anxieties deepened at the start of Jackson's second term in 1833, when Garrison and his friends organized the American Anti-Slavery Society, the first radical antislavery organization of its kind.

Over the next few years, the AA-SS, although never attracting more than a minority of northern whites, became a genuine mass movement, enlisting upwards of 250,000 members across the North by 1840. Apart from dispatching abolitionist lecturers on tours of churches and town meeting halls, the group (enlarging on the work of earlier activists who had opposed Indian removal) organized mass petition drives and flooded the Congress with memorials demanding the end of all federal support for slavery, including the abolition of slavery in the District of Columbia. Middling shopkeepers, farmers, and their families joined early, and the AA-SS soon widened its support to include substantial numbers of northern factory hands and artisan radicals; under Garrison's sway, large numbers of women, including thousands of ordinary wives and daughters as well as celebrated speakers such as the Quaker abolitionist Lucretia Mott, became involved; and a select number of wealthy Christian humanitarians, notably the brothers Arthur and Lewis Tappan, supplied the funds as well as the organizational acumen to support the distribution of abolitionist petitions and pamphlets and to help sponsor the abolitionist lecture tours. Leading northern black abolitionists either backed or cut their political teeth in the AA-SS; among the latter would be the escaped slave Frederick Douglass who, soon after his arrival in the North in 1838, would become a leading Garrisonian lecturer and writer.

As the abolitionist movement grew larger and more diverse, reactions against it, North and South, grew harsher. Beginning as early as 1822, in the aftermath of the Denmark Vesey affair, and with greater vigilance after Walker's pamphlet, the *Appeal*, appeared, southern legislatures enacted a variety of laws to impede the circulation of what they called "incendiary" antislavery materials. Stories abounded that slaveholders had offered to pay substantial bounties for the delivery to the South of various abolitionist notables, including Arthur Tappan, to give them the punishment they deserved. In the North, gentlemen Whigs as well as Jacksonians whipped up anti-abolitionist mobs that disrupted antislavery meetings, physically assaulted abolitionist speakers, and, in particularly severe outbursts in New York and Philadelphia, rampaged through black neighborhoods and destroyed white and black abolitionists' homes and businesses. (Only six months after Jackson left office, an anti-abolitionist mob in the Mississippi River town of Alton, Illinois, shot and killed the controversial abolitionist editor Reverend Elijah Lovejoy.)

When President Jackson was finally forced to deal directly with the abolitionists and their attackers, in 1835, he tried to contain the former without endorsing the latter—and without abdicating federal authority. The confrontation reveals the fine ambiguities and ultimate failures in Jackson's handling of slavery issues, and deserves detailed examination.

That year, the AA-SS undertook a new campaign to flood the southern mails with tracts calling for the immediate commencement of emancipation, in the hope of exercising moral suasion over the slaveholders while also reaching sympathetic free blacks and non-slaveholding whites. When the materials began arriving in Charleston, South Carolina, in July, Alfred Huger, the city's postmaster, a slaveholder and a Unionist during the nullification struggle, wrote to Amos Kendall, who had been selected but not yet confirmed as Jackson's new postmaster general. Huger was in a difficult situation, duty-bound as a federal official to deliver the mails, but also subject to South Carolina's ban on incendiary material. After pleading with Kendall to banish the mailings and asking for further instructions, Huger stuffed the abolitionist material in separate sacks and placed them under lock and key in his private office. When word got out, however, a band of leading Charlestonians, known informally as the Lynch Men, broke into Huger's office, stole the pamphlets, and later held a raucous public burning on the parade grounds adjoining the Citadel military academy.

Kendall, another slaveholder, sympathized with Huger and, in an open letter that was widely republished, stated that although he could neither condemn nor sanction what had occurred, there were certainly occasions when loyalty to the health and safety of one's local community must take precedence over federal law. Kendall ordered the Washington, D.C., postmaster to cease delivering any abolitionist materials or forwarding them to the South. He then told Jackson he wanted to halt the abolitionists' destructive mischief as quickly and as quietly as possible, and asked the president for directions about how to do so.

Jackson regarded the abolitionist effort disdainfully, much as he had the "free Missouri" campaign sixteen years earlier. He did not have the slightest doubt that the abolitionists were "guilty of the attempt to stir up amongst the South the horrors of a servile war." He was sure, as the Jacksonian *Globe* put it, that "[t]he Northern Bank Aristocrats" were behind the incitement, propelled by the belief that provoking "SLAVE EXCITEMENT" was "their only hope" to destroy the Democracy and reinstall the money power. Yet Jackson, defender of the laws as well as of the Missouri Compromise, also detested the anti-abolitionist mobs—especially, perhaps, the well-to-do mob ringleaders of nullifier Charleston. "This spirit of mob-law is becoming too common and must be checked," he told Kendall, "or ere long it will become as great an evil as servile war."[9]

With Congress out of session, Jackson advised strict obedience to the federal law by delivering the AA-SS materials, but only to those who had actually subscribed to them—which in Charleston would have been, at most, a tiny number of persons. He also suggested shaming any subscribers by publishing their names in the newspapers—a form of humiliation that Jackson seems not to have imagined as an invitation to further violence. Kendall, however, ignored the advice. Instead he established a policy of deferring to southern state and local regulations on the circulation of incendiary publications. Jackson disapproved of this forsaking of federal authority, but did nothing, preferring to let tempers cool until Congress reconvened. Then he would call for a new federal law that would make state and local regulations unnecessary by banning from the southern mails "incendiary publications intended to instigate the slaves to insurrection."[10]

If enacted, Jackson's proposal would have legalized federal censorship of the mails—another disgrace for his presidency. Yet even that proposal was too lenient for the most adamant southerners, including some inside Jackson's own cabinet. Secretary of State John Forsyth, a Georgian, complained to Van Buren that the administration was coddling the abolitionists, and suggested that the New Yorker might want to see to it that additional "mob discipline" befell the fanatics.[11] With the 1836 elections approaching, Van Buren, anxious as ever to sustain southerners' loyalties to the Democracy, took the advice seriously; and although the extent of Van Buren's involvement is unknown, New York Democrats did soon after organize a number of anti-abolitionist meetings, some of which degenerated into mob violence. John C. Calhoun, meanwhile, attacked Jackson's censorship call as soft on state rights and demanded a new federal law prohibiting delivery of offensive materials wherever state or territorial laws forbade it.

Finally, in July 1836, Congress passed a bipartisan, comprehensive postal law that rejected both Jackson's and Calhoun's proposals and upheld the government's commitment to deliver the mails. Formally, the abolitionists would appear to have carried the day. Yet southern officials, with Kendall's tacit approval, simply ignored the new law and did as they pleased. Jackson was appalled at the latest resistance to federal authority, but with his presidency drawing to a close, and mistrusting the federal courts to rule correctly, he too turned a blind eye. In effect, the controversy had produced an informal policy that would end up blocking abolitionist mail from being sent to the South until after the Civil War.

Jackson's effort to square the circle and censure both the abolitionists and their lawless attackers concluded in a glaring failure of leadership. The failure did not stem from Jackson's baleful views of the abolitionists. Those views were commonplace: even John Quincy Adams, then emerging as an antislavery hero, thought the

AA-SS pamphlets were "incendiary" and would "kindle the flames of insurrection."[12] Whig editors as well as Democrats advocated censorship of the abolitionist material and raised no complaints about anti-abolitionist violence like Jackson's. Yet Jackson let the situation get out of hand, then failed to enforce in full the 1836 Postal Act, thereby slighting the rule of law and suspending the jurisdiction of the federal government. Whatever his intentions were, Jackson ended up presiding over a policy in line with what the most insistent southern anti-abolitionists had desired all along.

In trying to suppress the problem of slavery in national politics, Jackson only worsened the problem. Southerners, including Calhoun, thought he had acted, once again, in bad faith. Northern Jacksonians, including the vociferous hard-money New Yorker William Leggett, thought Jackson and Kendall's handling of the mails controversy immoral and unconstitutional. "We cannot trample on the charter of our national freedom," Leggett charged, "to assist the slave-holder in his warfare with fanaticism." Soon enough, Leggett's anger, and a few others', would lead him to regard the abolitionists not as fanatics but as true egalitarians, advancing Jacksonian ideals beyond Jackson and the Democracy. That shift came, in part, because Jackson's efforts to silence the abolitionists only brought them more attention, as the righteous victims of suppression at the hands of self-described egalitarians. The paradox would worsen in years to come. "Instead of putting us down," one AA-SS official remarked, "[our opposers] put us and our principles up before the world—just where we wanted to be."[13]

At the height of the abolitionist mails battle, another political controversy over slavery exploded in Washington, this one involving Vice President Martin Van Buren more directly than President Jackson. Despite Van Buren's record of sympathy to southern rights (dating back to his support for Missouri's admission as a slave state), the nullification crisis and the rising contretemps over abolitionism had rendered all northerners dubious in some southerners' eyes. Jackson's firm endorsement of Van Buren for the presidency in 1836 was not enough to clear the air. Certain southerners pointed to Van Buren's past personal and political friendship with the late Rufus King, one of the leading antislavery spokesmen in the Senate during the Missouri crisis, and charged that the vice president had actually favored blocking slavery from Missouri. Others disliked him for his feud with Calhoun. "God knows I have suffered enough for my Southern partialities," Van Buren complained. "Since I was a boy I have been stigmatized as the apologist of Southern institutions & now forsooth you good people will have it that I am an abolitionist."[14] Administration insiders such as Secretary of State Forsyth tried to manipulate Van Buren to take an even harder pro-southern and anti-abolitionist line in advance of the 1836 campaign. Others, closer to Calhoun than to Jackson, tried to embarrass him.

James Henry Hammond, a young South Carolina editor and congressman, and one of Calhoun's confidants during the nullification crisis, saw that Van Buren might be undone with a parliamentary maneuver over the abolitionists' petition campaign before Congress. For years, southerners had suffered through the presentation of the obnoxious petitions on the floors of both the House and the Senate. The chances that the petitions would gain legislative results were nil, but they were a standing offense to the southerners' honor and opened up yet another possibility that antislavery talk might somehow reach the ken of slaves and stir up a rebellion. Late in 1835, Hammond had the idea of changing the rules of the House so that the abolitionist missives would automatically be turned away, without any consideration. (Calhoun tried unsuccessfully to fight for a similar change in rule in the Senate.) Southern honor would be protected—but northerners would be put on notice that they had to choose between upholding their own constituents' rights freely to petition Congress and securing the political loyalty of the South. The plan suddenly put Van Buren on the spot only months before he expected to gain the Democracy's presidential nomination.

Van Buren pulled out all the tricks that had earned him the nickname the "Little Magician." Trying to split the difference between self-protection and free speech, he devised a compromise plan that would receive the abolitionist petitions but automatically table them, thereby keeping slavery debates off the floor of Congress without, he claimed, abridging Americans' petitioning rights. The plan, he said, would "give the abolition question . . . its quietus," and preserve "the harmony of our happy Union."[15] Van Buren even persuaded a hitherto true-blue nullifier of noble lineage, Henry F. Pinckney of South Carolina, to introduce the measure.

Although branded a traitor by Hammond and other southerners, Pinckney would not back down, and Van Buren rallied his New York allies and other northern Jacksonians to support Pinckney's bill. On May 26, 1836—by which time Hammond had resigned his seat due to ill health—the House passed a slightly toughened version of Pinckney's bill. Roughly half the Whigs and other anti-administration congressmen, including most of Calhoun's South Carolina allies, abstained. The remainder voted "aye" along strongly sectional lines, the North in favor and the South opposed. A few northerners voted against the bill on strictly antislavery grounds, and others, conservative Whigs, joined them with hopes of shaming Van Buren in northern districts. Northern Democrats, and especially Van Buren's New Yorkers, voted overwhelmingly for the bill, seeing it as a compromise that supported neither abolitionists nor southern hard-liners.

Thanks to Van Buren, the House had muffled the pro-slavery side while subduing those sympathetic to abolitionism. In the short run—which, in the spring of 1836, is all that seemed to matter—this represented victory for Van Buren, Jackson, and the Jacksonian mainstream. But that success also sowed the seeds for future conflict. Southern hard-liners would revisit the petition issue and, by 1840, finally obtain the "hard" rule James Hammond had originally proposed. And throughout the late 1830s and early 1840s, a small band of antislavery northern Whigs, led by John Quincy Adams—who, after his presidential defeat in 1828, had won election to the House in 1830—conducted a running effort against any rule that shelved the abolitionist petitions. Their fight against the rule became the focus of congressional antislavery activity.

Adams, although opposed to slavery, thought the abolitionists dangerous radicals, and in 1835 he assured his Massachusetts supporters that he had no intention of getting caught up in what he called "the slavery and abolition whirligig." But the petition question disturbed him greatly as a violation of fundamental free speech rights, even in Van Buren's and Pinckney's softer proposal. Calling the rule flatly unconstitutional, Adams raised repeated objections, only to be met with catcalls from other congressmen and stern pronouncements by the speaker—Jacksonian James K. Polk—that he was out of order. "Am I gagged or not?" Adams demanded just before the House approved Pinckney's proposal in 1836, helping give the new rule its nickname before he acceded, temporarily, to the inevitable. Over the next eight years, Adams would lead the campaign against the "gag rule," heightening antislavery opinion until it was finally removed in 1844.

Shortly after his retirement from the presidency, Jackson read with dismay about his old foe Adams's continuing remonstrations against the Pinckney gag rule. "From his proceedings in congress," Jackson wrote, "he appears demented, and his actings and doings inspire my pity more than anger." Jackson became especially exercised over Adams's reading to the House an old letter, marked "Strictly Confidential," which, Adams purported, proved that Jackson had in 1830 connived in aiding a plot hatched by his old army friend Sam Houston to provoke a rebellion in the Mexican province of Tejas, supposedly to establish a new slave republic. In fact, the letter proved that Jackson had acted with restraint and probity. For Jackson, though, Adams's brandishing of a document that appeared to have been stolen was a low performance, the latest slight to Jackson's honor. Above all, Jackson thought that Adams's concern for the slaves was bogus and showed he was still a "hypocrite," posing as a humanitarian even though he was supremely interested in advancing his own political standing. "Humanity and charity toward him, would say that he must be demented," Jackson asserted, "if not, that he is the most reckless and depraved man living."[16]

Jackson was not simply bearing a grudge against his old adversary. As ever, he believed that antislavery agitation was insincere, aimed more at narrow political ends than at improving life for the slaves. And as ever, he believed such "reckless" and "demented" actions threatened to incite both murderous slave rebellions and the Union's dissolution. To the extent that the specter of slave insurrections filled Jackson's mind with horror, he was a typical slaveholder, and might even be counted as a pro-slavery man—except that, in the 1830s, the vast majority of white Americans, including the vast majority of antislavery northerners, blanched at the prospect of stirring a slave uprising. Rather, Jackson continued to approach slavery and abolition much as he had during the Missouri crisis, ever suspicious of narrowly personal and sectional motives, desiring above all to remove any political forces that might tear the nation apart.

The tragic limits of Jackson's perspective on slavery and antislavery, and those of the Democracy, were beginning to become apparent even as he fumed in the Hermitage—and they were beginning to divide the party. The New Yorker William Leggett, one of the foremost defenders of Jackson's banking and hard-money policies, grew increasingly disillusioned with the administration's stance on slavery issues and eventually called himself an abolitionist—heresy that New York's Democratic leaders punished by denying Leggett an expected nomination to Congress. Leggett would die prematurely in 1839, before his Jacksonian abolitionism amounted to much, but his close friend and sometime co-editor, the young lawyer Theodore Sedgwick III, would collect and republish Leggett's attacks on the anti-abolitionists and then himself become a leading antislavery voice among the Democrats. In Illinois, the outspoken Jacksonian Senator Thomas Morris, scourge of "the slave power," was denied reelection to the Senate by state party leaders and excommunicated from the Democracy—so Morris joined a tiny new political antislavery venture, the Liberty Party. In 1844, Morris would run for the vice presidency on the Liberty line; and four years later, after sectional strains had further rent the Democracy, none other than Martin Van Buren would head the national ticket of the schismatic Free Soil Party, successor to the Liberty Party and precursor of the Republican Party that emerged in 1854.

By that time, Jackson would be dead—and so would, for all intents and purposes, the Jackson Democracy of the 1830s, transformed into a new Democratic Party led by slaveholder partisans of southern rights and agreeable northerners still hoping to insulate politics from the by now inescapable fights over slavery. "All democracy left the democratic party," one veteran Jacksonian leader from Massachusetts observed, "and every true democrat that was too intelligent to be cheated by a name deserted its ranks." How Jackson would have reacted had he lived is, of course, open to debate. There is a case to be made that as a Tennessee slaveholder and Unionist, he would have adhered to the reborn Democracy. Certainly some of his closest political friends who did live long enough sided with the pro-slavery South, not least importantly Roger Brooke Taney, who as chief justice of the Supreme Court would, in 1857, write the flagrantly pro-slavery decision in the momentous case of *Dred Scott v. Sandford* that hastened the coming of the Civil War. Yet Jackson's old crony and adviser Francis Blair, a Republican convert and no longer editor of the *Globe*, contended that Jackson, too, would have switched to the Republicans, in order to battle the "perfect Southern phalanx" that, Blair charged, had "'sold out'" the Democracy "to Mr. Calhoun's nullifying party."[17]

There is more, though, to be gained from recognizing that by the 1850s, American politics had moved beyond the universe that had formed Andrew Jackson and which he had helped reshape. Concerned with the slavery issue only insofar as he could defuse it, Jackson, as president, saw democracy in very different and in some ways more constricted terms. At one level, Jackson envisaged democracy as a battle to heed and advance the interests and will of the free majority—the "humble members of society," the farmers, mechanics, and laborers of whom the Bank veto spoke—against monied privilege. At another level, Jackson's democracy aimed to protect the majority will and the nation from the blasphemy of nullification, and any other doctrines that encouraged disunion. The irony is that the more Jackson adhered to that democratic vision, the more he took actions that aggravated the sectional divisions he wished to contain.

Those ironies played out only in part over the political battles that arose directly from the rise of abolitionism and the southern slaveholders' responses. Jackson, like Jefferson before him, believed strongly in American expansionism and in widening what Jefferson called the empire of liberty. For most of his presidency, Jackson's involvement in foreign affairs revolved around his efforts to add new territories to the American dominion, while staving off what he considered constant and worrisome British efforts to undo the American Revolution. The foremost of these was the completion of Indian removal from the East, but Jackson's expansionist endeavors would also come to focus on the matter John Quincy Adams would later upbraid him about: the attempt by American settlers, in the region they called Texas, to win their independence from Mexican rule. Jackson proved a highly interested and passionate supporter of Texan liberty, with an eye to one day adding the vast region to the Union. But Jackson also quickly discovered that concerns over slavery had made the annexation of Texas—and westward expansion generally—an exceedingly thorny issue.

# 8

## Pushing Westward

The conclusion of the Napoleonic Wars in 1815, followed eight years later by the enunciation of the Monroe Doctrine, ended the intense American involvement in European power struggles that had played such a large role in the early Republic's politics. Conventional transatlantic foreign affairs thus proved a relatively minor concern of Jackson's presidency. Jackson's repudiation of various demands made by Adams for widening trade with the British West Indies caused only a temporary stir. More troublesome was Jackson's face-off with France over a treaty reached in 1831, whereby the French agreed to pay reparations for attacks made under Napoleon on American shipping. The French Chamber of Deputies refused to appropriate the funds; Jackson asked Congress to authorize retribution unless the money was paid; the bickering spiraled to the point where both nations recalled their ministers and a war seemed imminent; and Secretary of State Louis McLane resigned in protest at Jackson's aggressive stance. The French finally backed down, in line with British urgings, and the crisis ended without further consequences.

In place of its traditional Atlantic focus, American foreign policy became preoccupied with neighboring Mexico and a settler's uprising that had far-reaching implications for American domestic politics. Like his predecessor, Jackson yearned to acquire most of the north Mexican state of Coahuila y Tejas, whence considerable numbers of American farmers and large landowners (known as *empresarios*) had been moving for several years at the invitation of the Mexican government. Through the opening years of his second term, Jackson conducted a series of tortuous negotiations with Mexico that succeeded only in heightening Mexican apprehensions about the Americans' designs on the region. Those apprehensions would help spur a revolution that created an independent Texas republic—and considerable headaches as well as opportunities for Jackson and the Jacksonians.

Jackson's expansionist efforts also involved the completion of his Indian removal plans. The close-call passage of Jackson's removal bill did not end opposition to his policies. Instead, the main scene of conflict shifted to the federal courts, where the Cherokees, allied with white humanitarians, led the resistance to Jackson. The president, with his characteristic blend of iron will and political adroitness, finally got his way, but the process did not unfold as smoothly and benevolently as Jackson had expected. For those failures of Jackson's leadership, thousands of Indian men, women, and children paid with their lives.

The enactment of the Indian Removal Act in 1830 led to several bloody conflicts between the administration and the Indians, some of the worst of which occurred, ironically, outside the southwestern areas where the removals were heaviest. In 1832, members of the Sac and Fox tribes, led by Chief Black Hawk, moved eastward back across the Mississippi River to reoccupy land from which they had already been removed. In the three-month war that followed, American troops killed nearly six hundred Indians while enduring, by comparison, light casualties. Black Hawk surrendered. Three years later, renewed hostilities in Florida with the Seminoles, under Osceola, led to a vicious guerrilla war that lasted seven years, causing great suffering on both sides, until most of the surviving Seminoles were relocated.

The largest removals involved the Choctaws, Creeks, Chickasaws, and Cherokees. After 1830, the great majority of the Choctaws of Mississippi were sent to the West against their will (although in line with a treaty the government had extracted) and many met deaths from cholera and malnutrition. The Creeks, living in Alabama, signed an allotment treaty but many of them decided to stay, only to be besieged by speculators who defrauded them of their land and left them homeless. In desperation, the displaced turned to theft and even murder. Jackson's War Department sent troops to quell the disorder and forced fifteen thousand Creeks to emigrate. The Chickasaws in Mississippi, after waiting for western lands to be set aside for them, finally signed an allotment treaty in 1832, and by the end of 1837 five thousand of them had relocated across the Mississippi River.

The Cherokees fought back through the courts with the help of their white evangelical allies. As soon as Jackson's Indian Removal Act came into effect, the Georgia legislature declared all Cherokee laws null and void. On behalf of the Indians, William Wirt and the prominent ex-congressman John Sergeant (who became Henry Clay's running mate in 1832) filed an injunction asking the Supreme Court to overturn the Georgians' decision. The Court's eventual ruling in the case of *Cherokee Nation v. Georgia*, written by the aging Federalist Chief Justice John Marshall, appeared to favor the government by declaring that the Cherokees had no standing to sue. But Marshall based his reasoning on the proposition that the Cherokees were a "domestic dependent nation," an assertion that would come back to haunt the Jackson administration a year later.[1]

While it was busy nullifying all of the Cherokees' laws, the Georgia legislature also enacted one of its own, requiring all white persons to obtain a state license if they wished to live on Cherokee lands. Two Protestant evangelical missionaries to the Cherokees refused to comply, for which they were duly convicted and sentenced to four years at hard labor. Wirt, who had stepped forward as the Anti-Masons' presidential candidate in the 1832 election, and Sergeant appealed the conviction to the Supreme Court, and this time won their case—and a good deal more. Justice Marshall's decision in *Worcester v. Georgia* stated that since the Cherokees were "a distinct community," Georgia law had no effect over their territory; legal involvement with the Cherokees, rather, was limited to the federal government.[2] Georgians immediately protested that the Court had infringed on their state's sovereign rights.

According to an apocryphal story, Jackson reacted to Marshall's decision by declaring, defiantly, "Justice Marshall has made his decision. Now let him enforce it." The supposed remark, many writers have contended, typified Jackson's hair-trigger temper and outrageous disregard for any law that contradicted him. In fact, had Jackson actually delivered the rebuke, he would merely have been stating his insistent, democratic view that the judiciary was not supreme in its interpretation of the Constitution; that the president, as well as each member of Congress, had a sworn duty to uphold the Constitution as he understood it. As a coequal branch of the government, the executive could decide to disregard the Court's assertions. Far from idiosyncratic, this view was widely held: although the specific parties to a case were bound to obey the Court's decisions, and although the Court, like the president with his veto, could void specific pieces of legislation, the Court did not have the last word on larger constitutional issues. Four months after Marshall handed down the *Worcester* decision, Jackson would repeat this line of reasoning in his enormously popular Bank Veto Message. A quarter-century after that, Abraham Lincoln would offer it in his angry retorts to the majority decision in the *Dred Scott* case.

The *Worcester* ruling did, though, place Jackson in a difficult bind. The Court adjourned after Marshall announced his opinion, which gave Georgia authorities ten months, until January 1833, in which to respond. By then Jackson was embroiled in his struggle with the South Carolina nullifiers. Yet much as he did not want to relieve the pressure on the Cherokees to relocate or to provoke the Georgians into joining the South Carolinians as champions of state rights, neither did Jackson want to appear as if he were backing down to the Georgians; nor did he want to make anti-administration martyrs out of the two incarcerated missionaries. The White House prevailed upon Georgia governor Wilson Lumpkin to release the two men, and persuaded Wirt to agree not to file any more motions when the Court reconvened. The immediate crisis ended.

The struggle over Cherokee removal continued for another five years. In 1834, the War Department offered a removal treaty, but the majority of tribal chiefs refused to sign. At the head of the so-called anti-treaty party was Chief John Ross (one-eighth Cherokee by birth, and a former U.S. Army lieutenant who had fought the Creeks under Jackson), who had been elected the Cherokees' principal chief in 1828. In 1835, the Cherokee Nation as a whole overwhelmingly rejected the treaty in a tribal referendum; Governor Lumpkin sent in the militia to roust the anti-treaty Indians and arrest Ross. Released in December 1835, Ross journeyed to Washington to plead for better terms—but the pro-treaty party held a rump session of chiefs at New Echota and adopted a new removal agreement, which Jackson endorsed and the Senate later approved by a single vote. Given two additional years to prepare for their relocation, the Cherokees soon found themselves set upon by angry whites who tried to summarily drive them off their lands with clubs and whips. Jackson did not interfere, leaving the handling of violent lawlessness entirely in the hands of uncaring Georgia authorities.

Jackson remained absolutely convinced that removal was best for the Indians. By placing them under federal protection in the unorganized western territories, they would be spared the abuse they suffered in Georgia and elsewhere. One trouble with his position, of course, was that by the early 1830s it was manifestly clear that most of the Indians, especially the Cherokees, did not agree. Another problem was that Jackson proved unprepared to spend anywhere near the political and financial capital required to prevent the physical suffering that accompanied the demoralization of emigration. The policy that culminated in the Trail of Tears in 1838 was not genocidal. In completing the removal of the Indians to what he considered a safe haven, Jackson may well have spared them the obliteration that had been the fate of many northeastern tribes. But in order to save the Indians, Jackson's policy also destroyed thousands of them, and nearly destroyed many thousands more.

Further complicating the matter of American expansion, the region directly south of the territory Jackson had earmarked for the displaced Indians included the Mexican state of Coahuila y Tejas. Americans had long desired to obtain Tejas, all the more so after Mexico won its independence from Spain in 1821. In 1827, Adams's secretary of state, Henry Clay, authorized the American envoy to Mexico, Joel Poinsett (the South Carolina Unionist who would side with Jackson during the nullification crisis), to renegotiate the boundary between Mexico and the United States established by the Adams-Onís Transcontinental Treaty in 1819. Poinsett's efforts failed, but Jackson, as soon as he took office, personally instructed Poinsett's successor, Anthony Butler, to try again. Butler's penchant for shadowy intrigues and bribes, however, coupled with the vagueness of Jackson's instructions, raised the hackles of Mexican officials—as did the belligerence of Tejas's growing population of American émigrés.

Hoping to develop the sparsely populated region, the newly independent Mexican government agreed to sell up to four thousand acres to any new settler in exchange for minimal fees. The offer proved more attractive than the Mexicans had expected. Between 1821 and 1835, more than 35,000 Americans, mainly from the upper South and Arkansas Territory, settled in Tejas, many either bringing slaves or buying slaves after they had relocated. Mexican authorities tolerated the slaveholding, even after their government abolished slavery in 1829, but fears arose in Mexico City that the area was turning into a virtual province of the United States. In 1830 the government banned new immigration. Chafing at the restrictions and at the prospect of even greater intrusions by the central government in the future, the Tejas Americans drafted a constitution of their own in 1833. Two years later, after a military dictatorship under General Antonio López de Santa Anna took over the unstable Mexican government and rewrote the national constitution, the self-described Texans neared the brink of armed revolt.

In November 1835, following a skirmish between Mexican troops and American settlers in the town of Gonzales, a provisional Texan government formed in San Felipe de Austin. Four months later (with the full support of the region's greatest *empresario*, Stephen Austin, whom Santa Anna was holding in a Mexico City jail), a convention assembled in Washington-on-Brazos and signed a formal declaration of independence. Santa Anna took personal command of the army that marched north to crush the insurgency. On February 23, 1836, Santa Anna's main force, numbering twenty-five hundred troops, laid siege to the town of San Antonio de Bexar, where a group of just under two hundred Americans had holed up inside an old Franciscan mission known as the Alamo.

The Alamo's defenders included several interesting characters. Their commander, William Barrett Travis, was a South Carolina–born Alabama lawyer who had reputedly killed a man over infidelity with his first wife and had moved to Tejas in 1831—an illegal immigrant, according to Mexican law. James Bowie, a frontier drifter, knife designer, and Mexican citizen, contested Travis's command until illness and injury from a fall forced him to bed. The most famous defender, the Tennessean David Crockett, had arrived in Tejas less than two months before the siege, his political renown already well established. After serving under Jackson in the Creek War, Crockett was elected to Congress in 1827 as a Jackson supporter, only to break with him in 1831, switch to the emerging Whigs, and travel the lecture circuit as a rip-roaring, frontiersman backer of the Second Bank of the United States, until he was defeated for reelection in 1834. At the center of the Alamo's little garrison—and later of its mythic history—stood one of the first conservative populist celebrities in American history, a buckskin champion of Nicholas Biddle.

Santa Anna encircled the Alamo and crushed the resistance in an all-out assault on March 6 that took only about ninety minutes to complete. Sparing the insurgents' wives, children, and slaves, the general ordered that the rebels who had survived the fighting—including Crockett—be bayoneted and shot as pirates, to serve as an example to the rest of the Anglos. The Mexicans' victory was costly, though, and gained them little military advantage. Had Santa Anna awaited the arrival of his full artillery, he could have pulverized the mission's adobe walls and ended the resistance with relatively little loss of life on either side. But infuriated at the garrison's refusal to surrender, his sense of honor on the line, the general pushed for a rapid victory, winning what amounted to a massacre while also losing approximately six hundred of his own men. The truly important strategic target, meanwhile, lay to the southeast in the town of Goliad, the entryway to east Tejas, controlled by three hundred rebels commanded by Colonel James Fannin.

In mid-March, a much larger force of Mexicans, under General José de Urrea, overwhelmed Fannin's soldiers, most of whom, Fannin included, surrendered—only to be slaughtered, along with scores of other rebel prisoners, on direct orders from Santa Anna. A third American stronghold at San Patricio had fallen earlier in the month, and the Texan Revolution seemed doomed. But in trying to mop up the insurgency, Santa Anna divided his armies and left his main force vulnerable to attack. On April 21, about nine hundred rebels, commanded by President Jackson's close friend former Tennessee governor Sam Houston, surprised Santa Anna near Lynch's Ferry along the San Jacinto River and effectively destroyed his army. The next day, Santa Anna was captured trying to flee, dressed in an ordinary soldier's uniform, and at Houston's insistence, Santa Anna ordered all Mexican troops out of Tejas. In mid-May, in Velasco, the two sides signed two treaties, one public, one private, affirming Mexico's military withdrawal. Although not officially recognized by the Mexican government, the Republic of Texas was now, in effect, free and independent—open for recognition and (many Texans and Americans hoped) eventual annexation by the United States.

Euphoric Americans greeted the news of Houston's victory as a great triumph of freedom and enlightenment over the barbaric Mexicans. President Jackson was jubilant. At the very least, the new Republic of Texas would provide a buffer against the designs of Mexican militarists or any foreign power that might gain sway over the Mexicans to threaten American territory. At best, the new government might be amenable to allowing the United States to acquire Texas—or, as Jackson saw things, reacquire it. According to Jackson, Tejas had belonged to the United States under the terms of the Louisiana Purchase of 1803. Secretary of State John Quincy Adams, he contended, wrongfully bargained the region away to the Spanish in the Transcontinental Treaty of 1819. Although he would go through the motions of a formal annexation, Jackson hoped that the Texas rebels' success would restore to the United States an area that should never have been considered part of Mexico.

Going through the motions, however, would not be easy. The Mexicans suspected that Jackson had played a direct role in fomenting and then fortifying the Texas uprising. Any formal recognition of the new republic, let alone its annexation, would have to be handled delicately, and required negotiation with Santa Anna and the Mexican government. Domestic concerns were just as irksome. Although most Americans appeared to have been swept away by the victory of the underdog Texans, radical abolitionists and even some of the more measured northern antislavery men declared that the uprising was actually part of a sinister attempt to grab a huge parcel of land hospitable to slavery. Although the Texans had formed a single, unified republic, an annexed Territory of Texas could easily be carved up to create several new slave states— enough to give the slaveholders a permanent hammerlock over the U.S. Senate and dramatically increase the slaveholders' presence in the House of Representatives.

The veteran antislavery campaigner Benjamin Lundy led the attack on annexation. A peripatetic antislavery lecturer and editor of a newspaper he called *The Genius of Universal Emancipation*, Lundy had been William Lloyd Garrison's original mentor in the antislavery cause. Lundy had also spent considerable time in north Mexico, attempting to help resettle freed American slaves outside their slave-owning homeland. The experience persuaded Lundy that he was well acquainted with the rebels' hearts and minds. All of the Texan rhetoric about liberty and the rights of man, he charged, was spurious. In actuality, the uprising was part of a *"settled design"* to steal Tejas from Mexico and *"open a vast and profitable* SLAVEMARKET *therein."*[3]

Ordinarily, Jackson might have written off such criticism as the ravings of a sectional fanatic, out of touch with the American majority. But by the summer of 1836, a presidential campaign was under way, and Jackson did not want to make any precipitous move over Texas that might hamper the success of Martin Van Buren, whose election he regarded as a necessary vindication of his entire presidency. Lundy, moreover, had been gaining sympathy on the Texas issue from prominent and respectable men—including Congressman John Quincy Adams, only just beginning his involvement in the antislavery "whirligig." As president, Adams had tried to obtain Tejas peacefully from the Mexicans; now, he was convinced, Texas annexation was a pretext for expanding slavery. To Jackson, however, Adams's behavior appeared consistent: having given away the region to Spain in 1819, now Adams wanted to prevent its reacquisition. But no matter how Adams fit into the larger picture, the Texas question was too touchy to permit immediate bold action. Although he would extend formal recognition to the Texas Republic before he left office, Jackson would wait to do so until well after the election had been decided, and after Santa Anna paid him a personal visit in Washington. The matter of annexation would be left to his successors, who, Jackson hoped, could calm the sectional tensions that had disturbed the later years of his presidency.

. . .

Despite his past expansionist exploits and continued ambitions, Andrew Jackson did not add an inch of soil to the American dominion during his eight years in the White House. His presidency did bring, nevertheless, an important acceleration of the American push westward. The completion of Indian removal east of the Mississippi opened millions of acres of land to secure white settlement, from Michigan Territory in the North to the states and territories of the Deep South. The ensuing rise in those areas' populations led to the admission of two new states, Michigan and Arkansas, during the waning months of Jackson's second term. The success of the Texas Revolution presented the strong possibility of an enormous enlargement of American territory in the not too distant future.

The difficulties that surrounded these developments, especially in Texas, also reinforced the stresses that were afflicting the country and the Democracy by the mid-1830s. The results deepened the tragic dimensions of Jackson's presidency, especially in his second term. To Jackson, westward expansion was chiefly a nationalist and democratic enterprise: filling in Thomas Jefferson's empire of freedom, pushing back any possibility of Old World meddling in America's affairs, widening the opportunities for ordinary, virtuous, hardworking Americans to prosper much as he himself, a westward migrant of humble origins, had prospered. Jackson's vision of invigorated expansion was closely tied to his attacks on monied privilege over banking and the currency: opening lands, he wrote, to "actual settlers" and checking western speculation would curb the rise of a class of nonresident landlords and land jobbers, among "the greatest obstacles to the advancement of a new country and the prosperity of an old one."[4] His was a vision of western settlement as a patriotic and egalitarian fulfillment, free of strife, bloodshed, and the artificial hierarchies that Jackson believed had no place in a democratic republic.

The realities turned out to be much more difficult. Indian removal not only led to mass suffering and death, which Jackson had not anticipated, but it made possible the expansion of a cotton slave kingdom whose existence was offensive to some northerners. The Texas Revolution and the prospect of annexation further increased the possibilities for slavery's spread. Just as Jackson's suppression of nullification and his attack on the Second Bank of the United States alienated portions of the planter elite that the abolitionists charged he was indulging, his expansionist impulses contributed to a growth of slavery that heightened sectional tensions—and that darkened the impressions of some northerners, including some of his most ardent supporters, that his presidency had become entangled with the slave power.

As president, Jackson sensed that sectional politics directly threatened his party, the Constitution, and his hopes to secure a government based on the people's will. But he saw western expansion as an extension of those hopes—a national endeavor and an emollient on discord, not a ploy for spreading slavery. Shaped by his experiences during the American Revolution and the War of 1812, persuaded that the Missouri Compromise had settled the issue of slavery in the territories, he would never fully comprehend the political cross pressures aroused by the continued American thrust westward, or their potential destructiveness. When these pressures began to reshape politics in the mid-1830s, Jackson had already left his chief marks on the presidency and the nation, and his time was nearly done.

# 9

---

# Jackson's Legacy

On March 4, 1837, inauguration day, Andrew Jackson, his frame stooped and his presidency over, descended unsteadily from the Capitol to a waiting carriage amid loud cheering from the crowd below. Halfway down the steps, he halted, looked out over the throngs, and bowed in a gesture of humility as well as pride.

Jackson had won his final political battle by helping to secure Martin Van Buren's election. The Whig opposition, unable to mount a united national campaign, threw its support to three different regional candidates, only one of whom, the elderly ex-general from Ohio, William Henry Harrison, managed to win more than 10 percent of the popular vote. Although southerners' distrust of Van Buren did not abate, the Democrat ran well enough to carry most of the Deep South as well as most of New England and the crucial states of New York and Pennsylvania. The Jacksonians would enter their third consecutive term in the White House. They would also enjoy commanding majorities in the Senate and the House.

During the inauguration ceremony, Jackson watched with a renewed sense of vindication as another of his handpicked loyalists, Chief Justice Roger Taney, stepped forward to administer the oath of office to Van Buren. The wonder of Jackson's first inauguration eight years earlier was replaced by an atmosphere of continuity and confidence. Thomas Hart Benton later wrote that many inaugurations were filled with empty pageantry but Van Buren's "seemed to be reality—a real scene."[1]

Earlier in the day, Jackson, conscious of his place in history, issued a farewell address, written mainly by Chief Justice Taney, which emulated President George Washington's farewell of 1796. The message overflowed with Jackson's pleasure at what he considered his administration's greatest accomplishments: the destruction of the Second Bank of the United States, the suppression of nullification, and the completion of Indian removal. Jackson claimed that his presidency had resisted the workings of "[m]any powerful interests," protected the rights and liberties of "the great body of the people of the United States," and preserved popular sovereignty and the Union.[2]

Yet Jackson's valedictory, like Washington's, also warned of trouble ahead. Despite the successes of the Bank War, Jackson observed, "[t]he paper-money system and its natural associations—monopoly and exclusive privileges" had "struck their roots too deep in the soil," and the nation would have to redouble its strength to "eradicate the evil." Sectional wrangling persisted, caused by those who would "sow the seeds of discord between different parts of the United States . . . to excite the *South* against the *North* and the *North* against the *South*," over "the most delicate and exciting topics," by which Jackson meant slavery. Should the sectionalists ever sunder the country, Jackson's message said, "the controversies which are now debated and settled in the halls of legislation will then be tried in fields of battle and determined by the sword." Twenty years later, those words rang like prophecy.[3]

Coming to terms with Jackson's presidency is crucial to any understanding of American history. The presidents whom historians rate at the very top—Washington, Lincoln, and FDR—oversaw the three great political revolutions that have defined the American experience: the American Revolution and framing of the Constitution, the Civil War, and the New Deal. All three led the country through momentous wars and other tests of the nation's will. All three left behind national political institutions, including the presidency, very different than the ones they had inherited.

Jackson's presidency endured similar trials and wrought similar changes. More than any other American, Jackson oversaw the decline and fall of the elitist, gentry order established by the Framers, and its replacement with the ruder conventions and organization of democracy. More than any other president before him, he made the office of the presidency the center of action in national politics and government. Yet the incompleteness of Jackson's democracy—and the rise of two separate conceptions of democracy, North and South—contributed to the eventual disunion and terrible civil war he so deeply feared. And for many Americans, including the displaced Indians, Jackson's democracy and his activist presidency were disastrous. Questions thus linger over Jackson's contributions and leadership. What difference did he really make in the democratization of Americans' political sensibilities and practices? Given the terrible conflicts that followed, does his presidency deserve admiration or condemnation? Was he truly a democratic man of the people or a vengeful backwoods autocrat?

The widespread judgment that Jackson lacked a guiding political philosophy, and was motivated chiefly by his passions and prejudices, is as mistaken about the realities of the American presidency as it is about Jackson. True, Jackson was primarily a man of action who wrote nothing that approached a systematic political treatise and who appeared to shift his position in contradictory ways. Several accomplishments and declarations of which he himself was most proud were largely the handiwork of his aides and advisers. But the same holds true for all of the country's most revered presidents. Even Lincoln, the most eloquent president in American history, never presented a thorough account of what "Lincolnism" was, borrowed freely from his counselors, and often stood accused of inconsistency and vacillation. Jackson, like other effective presidents, developed his philosophy over time, in a series of pragmatic decisions and actions grounded in a few fundamental and unyielding principles. Like others, he surrounded himself with loyalists who presented him with diverse perspectives on political affairs, and he drew on their advice in order to refine his own thinking.

What some criticize in Jackson were actually traits of steadfastness and practicality that are advantageous to any political leader, especially in large and often divided democracies.

Jackson did have a more volatile personality than most other presidents, and was quick to personalize political disputes and see himself encircled by dark conspiracies. In this respect, he bears a superficial resemblance to many failed chief executives, including, in recent times, Richard M. Nixon. Jackson's fiery temperament, coupled with his capacity for intense distrust that sometimes turned into obsession, distracted him from the nation's business during the Eaton affair, and nearly crippled his first term. But Jackson righted himself and his administration in 1830 and 1831. Thereafter, his search for personal success and absolution merged with the "task of *reform*" he had proclaimed in 1829, both in advancing changes such as rotation in office and in meeting new contingencies, above all during the Bank War and the nullification crisis.

Jackson outlined the essential ideas of what became known as Jacksonian Democracy in piecemeal fashion throughout his presidency. One of the fullest, simplest, and most direct statements came in a letter he wrote to his ward Andrew Jackson Donelson in 1835. Jackson posed the question: What distinguishes "Whigs, nullies & blue light federalists" from Democrats? He began with specific matters of policy: Democrats opposed a national bank, supported rotation in office, and favored limited state and national government according to a strict reading of the state and federal constitutions. But Jackson then moved to more abstract ideas about government. Democrats, he wrote, subscribed to "the republican rule that the people are the sovereign power, the officers their agents." Above all, they were "true republicans agreeable to the true Jeffersonian creed."[4]

These might sound like partisan platitudes today, but in Jackson's time they articulated important and by no means settled axioms of democratic government. The Constitution had provided for a national government based on popular sovereignty, a term that, to Jackson, meant precisely what it said, the rule of the people.

The people had the right to expect their representatives to voice and advance their will. The people decided government's actions, according to majority rule. The people's representatives were to neither decide for themselves what the people's will actually was nor ignore it in order to advance their own desires and beliefs. No government body, including the Supreme Court, could supersede the popular majority, as expressed in elections, least of all on matters concerning the true meaning of the Constitution. No private interests could be permitted to obtain special privileges that would bend the Constitution to fulfill their own selfish interests, over and above those of the people.

These ideas—at odds with those of such wide-ranging adversaries as John Quincy Adams, William Lloyd Garrison, Nicholas Biddle, and John C. Calhoun—undergirded all of President Jackson's major efforts. The Bank veto and the war on the Bank hung on Jackson's insistence on dismantling a tremendously powerful private institution that evaded democratic checks and balances. Jackson's attack on nullification grew from his claim that the nullifiers were defying both the explicit terms of the Constitution and the people's will—heeding Calhoun's heretical claim that "[c]onstitutional government, and the government of the majority, are utterly incompatible"—and directly threatening the Union. Jackson's rejection of the Cherokees' claims to tribal sovereignty and his pursuit of Indian removal rested partly on his belief that creating separate nations within the borders of the United States violated the Constitution, permitted the federal government to violate state sovereignty, and created an abnormal and intolerable threat to national integrity and security.

Who, then, did Jackson envisage as "the people"? Not black Americans, the preponderance of them enslaved; not American women, of any class or color, who lacked basic political and civil rights; and certainly not the Indians. Neither, though, did he equate the American people, as many scholars have claimed he did, with the nation's rising businessmen and expectant capitalists, who wanted to liberate business from a corrupt government and institute a policy of laissez-faire. It is true that Jackson believed that a large and expansive federal government was oppressive and had no legitimate powers to intercede with the natural flow of human commerce and individual self-advancement. But in the 1830s (unlike in our own time) this meant liberating democratic government from the corrupting encroachments of powerful business. Jackson stood up, in the people's name, against the *"few Monied Capitalists"* to free government from "the rich and powerful" and their "selfish purposes." Thus Jackson was sometimes prepared to give the government more power, not less, in overseeing finance and the nation's economy.

"The people," for Jackson, were always "the humble members of society," as he described them in the Bank Veto Message. They were the "working classes of Americans," he later wrote, "the laboring classes" and their families—who lacked political connections and who rose or fell by dint of their talents and hard work. "The agricultural, the mechanical, and the laboring classes have little or no share in the direction of the great moneyed corporations," his farewell message declared:

> The planter, the farmer, the mechanic, and the laborer all know that their success depends upon their own industry and economy, and that they must not expect to become suddenly rich by the fruits of their toil. [T]hese classes of society form the great body of the people of the United States; they are the bone and sinew of the country. . . . But . . . they are in constant danger of losing their fair influence in the Government, and with difficulty maintain their just rights against the incessant efforts daily made to encroach upon them . . . [by] the moneyed interest.

With his banking and currency policies, Jackson tried to protect ordinary American citizens from government favoritism to the rich and powerful. He strove to establish an alternative form of democratic commerce, one that would not, first and foremost, serve the well-being of merchants and financiers. That alternative system, based on hard money, would, he believed, open the way to a moderate but secure prosperity for most Americans, while shielding them from the hurtful boom-and-bust cycles endemic to what the Jacksonian *Globe* called a system of speculation based on "a succession of rolls of the dice."[5]

In his pursuit of egalitarian reform, Jackson pushed certain ideas of popular democracy as far as any president has—further, perhaps, than the United States could possibly sustain, now as well as then. He began with the presumption that the actual governing of the country should be conducted by the people at large, striking down elitist presumptions with his proposals for rotation in office. Elected officials, including the president and U.S. senators, he contended, should be elected directly by the voters, not by an Electoral College or the state legislatures. By the end of his presidency, he even favored popular election of the federal judiciary and the imposition of seven-year terms on federal judges (though with provisions that would permit their reelection). Whereas in aristocratic Britain an independent judiciary was necessary to ward off impositions by the crown and the nobility, in democratic America "the people would always re-elect the good judges."[6]

Some of Jackson's proposals, notably the direct election of senators, were well ahead of their time.* Others remain open to serious questions, including whether maximizing direct electoral control over federal officials might hamper deliberative government. Too much direct democracy, critics charge, would dangerously subject public officials to passing popular whims or enthusiasms, while providing insufficient legal safeguards for minorities and for unpopular views. These debates over the pros and cons of direct democracy

---

*Direct popular election of the Senate would not be secured until the ratification of the Seventeenth Amendment to the Constitution in 1913.

are a perennial feature in American politics. Over the long run, more constrained conceptions of democracy have proven an indispensable check on a potentially tyrannical majority. But more expansive democratic ideas have been a powerful solvent of privilege and stagnation, and Jackson deserves a great deal of the credit for injecting them into the American political tradition. Although he did not fit the mold of a philosopher-statesman, he certainly had a strong democratic political philosophy, and carried it as far as he could.

Jackson's forceful style, as well as his ideas, also established the foundations of the modern democratic presidency. By the time he departed the White House, Jackson had twice recomposed his cabinet, ostracized one vice president and selected his successor, and vetoed more legislation than any of his predecessors combined (and more than any later president until the Reconstruction era). His assertions of presidential prerogative altered Americans' presumptions about the president's role in the national government. Jackson's staunch opponent Benjamin Watkins Leigh observed that "[u]ntil the President developed the faculties of the Executive power, all men thought it inferior to the legislature—he manifestly thinks it superior." Although overstated, Leigh's assessment was basically correct.[7]

The republican ideas inherited from the Revolution, and reinforced by the Revolution's anti-monarchism, held that the legislative branch, and in particular the lower house of the legislature, was more directly representative of the people than the executive. Jackson, although still positing the equality of the three coordinate branches of government, reversed that premise. Especially now that the voters, and not state legislatures, chose presidential electors (the lone exception, after 1828, being aristocratic South Carolina), the president, along with the vice president, was the most direct individual embodiment of the majority will. Congressmen represented only their small districts, and senators their states; the president represented the entire electorate and was thus, Jackson said, more "amenable to the people." To Whigs such as Leigh, Jackson was an anti-democrat out to augment "the monarchical part of Government." Jackson, however, perceived the American executive as a uniquely democratic part of government, an idea that would later animate Theodore Roosevelt, who wrenched the office out of the throes of what one of his successors, Woodrow Wilson, called "congressional government," and help establish the presidency as we know it.

Jackson and his supporters also created the first mass democratic national political party in modern history. Earlier semblances of American political parties had emerged over sharp ideological differences and then devised innovative means to spread their messages and get their voters to the polls. Yet to the generation of Jefferson and John Adams, the very idea of parties still remained suspect as vehicles of personal ambition and fomenters of disunion. And although popular involvement, especially at the state level, increased after 1800, power in national politics still remained concentrated in the hands of a fairly small elite. When, in 1801, President Thomas Jefferson proclaimed, in a conciliatory fashion, that "we are all republicans, we are all federalists," his aim was not to legitimize the existence of two permanent political parties; rather, he later wrote, he wanted to sink Federalism "into an abyss" by absorbing the more moderate Federalists into his own Republican Party and delegitimizing the rest, thereby ending, for good, all party strife. Only decades later, after the Panic of 1819 and the Missouri crisis shook the one-party politics that arose after the Federalists' demise, did Jefferson come to understand that party divisions might be ineluctable. Yet even then, the older generation assumed that national party affairs would still be conducted by supposed natural aristocrats, through devices like the nomination of presidential candidates by congressional caucus.[8]

The Jackson Democracy did not fully reconcile itself to what later historians would describe as a mature party system. In correcting what they considered the insidious opportunism and factionalism that beset one-party politics, the Jacksonians also considered themselves the only authentic successors of the Jeffersonian Republicans and, thus, of the Revolution itself. Their opponents— neo-Tories, they believed, at war with the Spirit of 1776—should be allowed to organize their own party and contest free and democratic elections. But these contests, the Jacksonians thought, would serve mainly as a spur to their own party faithful, to keep them disciplined and sharpen their devotion, as they put it, to the success of principles, not men. They fully expected that they, the party of popular sovereignty, would hold power most of the time, unless, as Martin Van Buren wrote, a slackening of zeal and vigilance caused "the gradual abandonment of the principles it sustained."[9]

Within those limitations, though, the Jackson Democracy enlarged greatly on earlier forms of party organization. In place of discarded state and national nominating caucuses, the Jacksonians built a network of party committees that stretched from the ward and township levels to the quadrennial national convention. Political activities would continue more or less year-round, focused on the lowliest local contests as well as on presidential elections, with party committees calling regular meetings to approve nominations and pass resolutions. Party newspapers, from the *Globe* in Washington to the local sheets, would publicize these events and keep the faithful apprised of the latest news—and of the proper way to assess that news. At election times, the party machinery would reach into high gear, sponsoring elaborate campaign rallies, dinners, and processions in order to raise funds and heighten party morale. And, although designed to fit the image of Andrew Jackson's own politics, the Democracy was larger than any individual, even its hero. The coalition formed in advance of Jackson's 1828 election evolved, over the next eight years, into the kind of party that Jackson's loyalist Martin Van Buren had foreseen in his famous letter to Thomas Ritchie—emerging just in time, after political twists and turns he could not have predicted, to elect Van Buren president in 1836.

Jackson retired, all but spent, to his mansion, horses, slaves, and the tomb of his beloved Rachel. His health had been wretched for decades. More than once during his presidency, the effects of old war and dueling wounds, of the chronic dysentery he had contracted during the Creek Wars, and of a lifetime spent smoking and chewing tobacco laid him so low that many feared he would not survive. The white-haired master of the Hermitage returned home wracked by a persistent cough, severe pains on his left side, chronic blinding headaches, and recurrent insomnia. Although he was still strong enough to take his stallion Sam Patch for turns around his holdings, the horse racing, gambling, and other gentlemanly sports that once filled his leisure time no longer held his interest. Never an especially pious man (despite his mother's wishes and his wife's intense devotion), he joined the Presbyterian Church in 1838—although initially he balked when his minister told him he needed to absolve, in his heart, all his old enemies.

Politics remained his chief passion. When the long-predicted financial panic finally struck in May 1837, Jackson strongly urged President Van Buren to stay the course of hard-money policies. The new president had reasons of his own, but Van Buren's decisions not to rescind the Specie Circular and to ask Congress to establish a so-called Independent Treasury, thereby achieving a divorce of the government and commercial banking, pleased Jackson immensely. Keeping close tabs on developments in Washington, he scorned the Whigs (whom he sometimes called "Federalists," using what he thought the only proper term) and their Conservative Democratic allies as vile enemies of "the labor of the country." When the treasury bill finally passed Congress in 1840, Jackson rejoiced: "The Whiggs whipt, so it goes *all well.*" The Whig effort later that year to proclaim themselves the true democrats—and replace Van Buren with William Henry Harrison in their famous Log Cabin and Hard Cider campaign—struck Jackson as both disgraceful and desperate. "I have all along assured [our opponents]," he wrote to Van Buren at the end of July, "that the Federalist hard cider drinkers . . . would not carry a state in the union south or west of the potomac but one and that doubtfull, *Kentucky.* I am now persuaded my prediction will be realised."[10]

Jackson's howls of disappointment at Harrison's crushing victory passed quickly when Harrison died only a month after his inauguration. Jackson made no attempt to hide his satisfaction at the sudden interference by a "kind and overruling providence" to keep Harrison, "under the direction of the profligate demagogue, Henry Clay," from undoing all of his and Van Buren's hard-won achievements.[11] Yet the disarray that followed—with a state rights Whig, John Tyler, elevated to the presidency and pitted against his great rival Henry Clay—spelled trouble for a return in 1844 to the Jacksonian status quo ante. Goaded by state rights southerners, Tyler pushed for the annexation of Texas, reopening sectional divisions over slavery and expansion; the divisions worsened when Tyler's secretary of state, John C. Calhoun, made Texas annexation an issue of southern rights on explicitly pro-slavery grounds. The 1844 election was approaching, and Clay, the expected Whig nominee, had already opposed the annexation drive. His expected opponent, a resurgent Martin Van Buren, faced a difficult choice. Having hoped to keep the Texas issue out of the election, angered by what he saw as Calhoun's latest attempt personally to do him in, and wary of losing the bulk of the northern vote, Van Buren was inclined to oppose Texas annexation. But doing so, he well knew, would so alienate southern Democrats that he might not even receive the nomination.

Jackson, who had long coveted Texas, supported its annexation, although for reasons very different from Calhoun's. Jackson's old expansionist hopes had become linked to his ancient fear and loathing of the British. During the early 1840s, Britain had become increasingly entangled in the Texas issue, trying to forestall American annexation by enticing the Texans with a variety of financial incentives and by offering to persuade Mexico finally to recognize the independent republic. To Calhoun and the southern state rights men, the British had an ulterior abolitionist motive: in gaining recognition from Mexico, the stories ran, Texans would have to agree to free their slaves. Jackson, however, was convinced that the British were intent on reconquering America, using Texas as a base of operations for seizing control of the Mississippi Valley and the Gulf of Mexico as they had failed to do—thanks to Jackson—in 1814 and 1815. Texas, he wrote to Francis Blair, was "the important key to our future destiny—take and lock the door against all danger of foreign influence."[12]

The 1844 campaign was Jackson's last. When Van Buren, in the most courageous act of his political career, came out in opposition to Texas annexation, Jackson threw his support to his loyal friend and follower from Tennessee, the former Speaker of the House, James K. Polk. As Van Buren's backers had feared, their man's stand on Texas cost him the nomination, and the Democratic convention deadlocked over a candidate. Finally, Polk emerged the winner, the first "dark horse" presidential nominee in American history. Jackson backed Polk to the hilt, playing the part of elder statesman of the party, and enhancing Polk's chances by convincing President Tyler, abandoned by the Whigs, not to mount a third-party campaign that might well siphon off valuable southern Democratic votes.

Polk won a narrow victory over Jackson's old nemesis Henry Clay. Jackson had been his chief political benefactor—and, in the process, Jackson helped assure the annexation of Texas, and, in time, a worsening of sectional hatreds. Yet neither Jackson nor Polk saw the situation in those terms. While calling for the addition of Texas, the Democratic platform and the Polk campaign also demanded the addition of Oregon, an area now filling up with American settlers, its border with Canada the subject of hot contestation between the United States and Great Britain. Texas annexation, by Jackson's and Polk's lights, was part of a national enterprise, not (contrary to Calhoun) a sectional cause or (contra to the abolitionists) a pro-slavery ruse.

Jackson's pride in Polk would, however, rapidly diminish. After pausing to visit Jackson at the Hermitage on the way to his inauguration, the president-elect, now known by the nickname "Young Hickory," listened patiently to Old Hickory's advice about policies and appointments. But as soon as he surveyed the political situation in the capital, Polk went his own way, naming none of Jackson's favorites to the cabinet and replacing the Jacksonian warhorse Francis P. Blair as editor of the administration's official newspaper (which, under the direction of Thomas Ritchie, was renamed the *Union*). Jackson, aghast, worried that Polk's precipitate moves might damage party unity. But Polk would not budge. He was determined, he wrote, "to be *myself* President of the U.S."[13]

All along, Jackson was dying, as fast as he could get on with it, he told one friend. Although he continued, as he had for years, to receive strangers who just wanted to tell the world they had met Andrew Jackson, his body became severely bloated in the early spring of 1845, as one organ after another began to fail. Friends and family gathered at his bedside. His last words, those of a plantation patriarch, were directed at a group of his slaves who were weeping out on the porch. "Oh, do not cry—be good children & we will all meet in heaven."[14] At six in the afternoon on June 8, he died. Two days later, he was buried in the Hermitage garden tomb next to Rachel.

Democracy's ascendancy was Jackson's greatest triumph—the supreme reason why his legacy retains its luster. Yet the tragedies of Jackson's presidency were also numerous and enormous and need to be weighed in the balance. In his zeal to extend a paternal hand to the Indians, Jackson promulgated a coercive and fiscally tight policy that invited fraud and caused immense suffering and the deaths of thousands. His detestation of nullification prompted a forceful response that crushed the immediate threat posed by Calhoun's assertions of unlimited state sovereignty and permissible secession, but that response also alienated large numbers of southern planters and fostered sympathy for the nullifiers. His attempts to suppress the abolitionists in order to buttress national harmony led him to propose a federal censorship law that belied his democratic professions, angering some members of his own party and further inflaming sectional divisions. In the endeavor on which he wagered his entire presidency, he successfully battled the Second Bank of the United States, and thereby permanently changed the nation's political economy. Never again would formal control over banking and currency policy fall so far from democratically elected leaders as they had under Nicholas Biddle's Bank of the United States. But Jackson's efforts to establish a suitable replacement for the Bank, and to fight his adversaries' attempts to obstruct those efforts, contributed to a financial crisis that would make life miserable for President Martin Van Buren—and pave the way for the Whigs to win the presidency.

The most powerful contradictions generated by Jackson's presidency and legacy had to do with slavery, democracy, and American expansionism. For Jackson, as it had been for Thomas Jefferson, the nation's physical growth was a precondition for the continued prosperity of those Americans he considered the sum and substance of "the people," the great majority of farmers, artisans, and laborers. With fresh land, and with protection from the monied few, the many would have the chance to establish their personal independence, provide themselves and their families with at least a decent prosperity, and enlarge the American experiment in free government. Yet the push westward of rival political and social systems— one based on free labor, the other on chattel slavery—would reignite the sectional furies that the Missouri Compromise had temporarily contained and settled. In the debates over the annexation of Texas and the fate of newly acquired lands beyond the domain of the Louisiana Purchase, American expansionism would bring not renewed amity and national resolve, but ferocious conflicts about whether slavery was essential to democratic government or was democracy's undoing.

As Jackson noted in his farewell address, sectional divisions over slavery and democracy directly threatened his very conception of democracy. For Jackson, the confrontations were artificial, whipped up by ambitious demagogues in order to distract the electorate from the truly important division between the privileged few and the humble many. But slavery and its expansion were not artificial issues; they were redefining how Americans thought about the few and many; and these clashing views cut to the heart of how Americans thought about democracy. How long could Jackson's Democracy, in the name of preserving the Union, back the gag rule and other attacks on free speech without, in northerners' eyes, fatally compromising their professed dedication to equality? How long could the Jacksonians portray themselves as the party of "the laboring classes" and still tolerate slavery and the political domination of slaveholders—men who, the hard-money Jacksonian Thomas Morris of Ohio declared, lived upon "the unrequited labor of others"?[15] Alternatively, how long, growing numbers of southerners wondered, could equality be preserved unless the Democracy took more dramatic steps to preserve what they considered the foundation of equality and democracy among free men, the institution of black slavery? How long could democracy endure with slavery under assault—and without the Democracy declaring that slavery, condoned by the Framers, was the cornerstone of democratic government?

Two decades would pass before the clash between the northern democracy and the southern democracy shattered Jackson's Democratic Party in all but its name. Yet in the most profound irony of all, the widening of democratic politics that (as Herman Melville would later write in *Moby-Dick*) "didst pick up Andrew Jackson from the pebbles" and "thunder him higher than a throne" would also render that conflict irrepressible. By expanding popular politics and enshrining the popular will, Jackson and his followers exposed the political system to precisely the kinds of agitation they (and their Whig Party adversaries) hoped to keep forever out of national debates. Using all of the electioneering techniques pioneered by the Jackson Democrats, new movements, factions, and parties would arise and amass popular support over issues connected to slavery—and would elect candidates to national office dedicated solely to addressing whether slavery threatened or embodied democratic values. Less than four years after Jackson's farewell, the Liberty Party, the nation's first explicitly antislavery political party, initiated its first presidential campaign; four years later, it would run another presidential ticket, lambasting the slave power as "an overwhelming political monopoly" that had "subverted the constitutional liberties of more than 12,000,000 American freemen."[16] Southern fury at such charges helped fortify backing for a powerful southern state rights faction within an increasingly unstable Democracy. That faction, led by John C. Calhoun, would force the slavery issue front and center in 1844 over the annexation of Texas.

Jackson lived long enough to feel these early tremors of the crisis of American democracy over slavery, and he would try to still them with all the strength he could muster. He would never fully comprehend how his own democratic achievements had brought them about, and lead his countrymen, North and South, to begin questioning whether democracy could endure in a nation half slave and half free, a house divided against itself.

A little more than two months before he died, Jackson wrote a letter to Jesse Duncan Elliott, another aging veteran of the War of 1812. Near the end of his remarks, Jackson observed that "[t]rue virtue" could reside only "with the people, the great laboring and producing classes . . . the bone and sinew of our confederacy."[17]

It was, in a way, a fitting valedictory, a condensation of what had become the straight Jackson political line during the 1830s. That line had become snarled around issues concerning slavery and expansion—issues that raised upsetting questions about true virtue, the people, and democracy and would tear apart both Jackson's party and the Union he loved.

But that these issues arose at all was, paradoxically, in part to Jackson's credit, much as he strove to suppress them in order to preserve the nation's peace. By pushing the idea of democracy as far as he did, and by equating the Union's survival with the survival of free government, Jackson expanded the terms upon which Americans conducted the national experiment in popular sovereignty. As president, he established democratic and nationalist principles that have endured to this day. If his own standards of equality and justice fall beneath our own, he helped make it possible for today's standards and expectations to be as elevated as they are. His tragedies are undeniable. So are his triumphs and his greatness.

# Notes

The following abbreviations appear in the notes:

AC              *Annals of Congress,* 1789–1824
CAJ             John Spencer Bassett, ed., *Correspondence of Andrew Jackson* (Washington, D.C.: The Carnegie Institution, 1926–1935)
CG              *Congressional Globe,* 1834–71
PAJ             Sam B. Smith, Harriet Chappell Owsley et al., eds., *The Papers of Andrew Jackson* (Knoxville, Tenn., 1980– )
RD              *Register of Debates in Congress,* 1824–37
Richardson      James D. Richardson, ed., *A Compilation of the Messages and Papers of the Presidents* (Washington, D.C.: Bureau of National Literature and Art, 1910)

PROLOGUE: JACKSON AND THE AGE
OF THE DEMOCRATIC REVOLUTION

1. James G. Barber, *Andrew Jackson: A Portrait Study* (Washington, D.C.: Smithsonian Institution, 1991), 123–24.
2. James Parton, *Life of Andrew Jackson* (New York: Mason Brothers, 1860), 3:554.
3. Bayard Tuckerman, ed., *The Diary of Philip Hone, 1828–1851* (New York: Dodd, Mead, 1889), 1:96–97; quotation in Arthur M. Schlesinger, Jr., and Fred Israel, eds., *History of American Presidential Elections* (New York: Chelsea House, 1985), 2:509.
4. James C. Curtis, *Andrew Jackson and the Search for Vindication* (Boston: Little, Brown, 1976); Andrew Burstein, *The Passions of Andrew Jackson* (New York: Alfred A. Knopf, 2003), quotation on p. 237. For a fuller listing of the relevant literature, see Selected Bibliography.

5. Richardson, 2:1011; William Cobbett, *The Life of Andrew Jackson, President of the United States of America* (London: Mills, Jowett, and Mills, 1834), iv; Wright quoted in Celia Morris Eckhardt, *Fanny Wright: Rebel in America* (Cambridge, Mass.: Harvard University Press), 253; Theodore Sedgwick, Jr., *A Collection of the Political Writings of William Leggett* (New York: Taylor & Dodd, 1840), 1:70; Kent quoted in John Theodore Horton, *James Kent: A Study in Conservatism, 1763–1847* (New York: D. Appleton-Century), 308.
6. The phrase is borrowed from R. R. Palmer's classic two-volume work, *The Age of the Democratic Revolution: A Political History of Europe and America, 1760–1800* (Princeton, N.J.: Princeton University Press, 1959–64). I believe instead of halting in 1800, there is more use in viewing the period from 1776 to 1848 as a coherent era, roughly along the lines argued in another classic work, E. J. Hobsbawm, *The Age of Revolution, 1789–1848* (Cleveland: World Publishing, 1962). Unlike Hobsbawm, who concentrates on Britain and Europe, I think that the American Revolution and not the French signaled the period's political upheavals.
7. Richardson, 1:310.
8. Seward to Thurlow Weed, April 12, 1835, in Seward, *William H. Seward: An Autobiography from 1801 to 1834* (New York: Derby and Miller, 1891), 1:258.
9. Jackson to Willie Blount, January 4, 1813, in *CAJ*, 1:254–55.
10. "Division Orders, October 24, 1813," in *CAJ*, 1:337–38; Jackson quoted in Robert V. Remini, *Andrew Jackson and the Course of American Empire, 1767–1822* (New York: Harper & Row, 1977), 233.

1: A ROARING FELLOW

1. William L. Saunders, ed., *The Colonial Records of North Carolina* (Raleigh, N.C.: P. M. Hale, 1886–90), 8:75–80.
2. Jackson quoted in Marquis James, *Andrew Jackson: The Border Captain* (Indianapolis: Bobbs-Merrill, 1933), 31.
3. Parton, *Jackson*, 1:104.
4. Gallatin quoted in ibid., 196. Parton borrowed the remark from Richard Hildreth, a powerful Whig writer who had little affection for Jackson. Although Parton did not challenge the quotation's authenticity, he called the description inaccurate, a product of Gallatin's faulty memory and his distaste for Jackson.
5. Ibid., 212.
6. Jackson to James Robertson, January 11, 1798, in *CAJ*, 1:42.
7. "To the Troops, October 24, 1813," in *CAJ*, 1:338.

8. Crockett, *The Life of Davy Crockett by Himself,* ed. Curtis C. Davis (1834; New York: New American Library, 1955), 46.

9. Jackson quoted in Remini, *Jackson and the Course of American Empire,* 233.

10. Vincent Nolte, *Fifty Years in Both Hemispheres; or, Reminiscences of the Life of a Former Merchant* (New York: Redfield, 1854), 209–10.

11. Parton, *Jackson,* 2:208–09.

12. "Jackson's Address to His Troops on the Right Bank, January 8, 1815," in *CAJ,* 2:136.

13. *The Times* (London), December 30, 1814, quoted in Henry Adams, *History of the United States of America during the Administrations of Thomas Jefferson and James Madison* (1889–91; New York: The Library of America, 1986), 2:1220.

14. Jackson to Robert Hays, February 9, 1815, in *CAJ,* 2:162.

2: "JACKSON AND REFORM"

1. Charles Francis Adams, ed., *Memoirs of John Quincy Adams, Comprising Portions of His Diary from 1795 to 1848* (Philadelphia: Lippincott, 1874–77), 5:128.

2. Monroe to Andrew Jackson, December 28, 1817, Monroe Papers, New York Public Library.

3. Jackson to Monroe, June 2, 1818, Monroe Papers, New York Public Library.

4. *AC,* 15th Cong., 2nd sess., 631–55, quotation on p. 655; *American State Papers: Military Affairs* (Washington, D.C.: Gales and Seaton, 1832), 1:743.

5. Franklin (Tennessee) *Gazette,* July 17, 1818, quoted in Remini, *Jackson and the Course of American Empire,* 375.

6. On Jackson and banking issues in these years, see especially Charles Grier Sellers, Jr., "Banking and Politics in Jackson's Tennessee," *Mississippi Valley Historical Review* 61 (1954): 61–84.

7. Adams, ed., *Memoirs,* 5:128–29.

8. Kim Tousley Phillips, "William Duane, Revolutionary Editor," Ph.D. diss., University of California at Berkeley, 1968, 569, 576.

9. *Mercantile Advertiser* (Mobile, Ala.), January 28, 1824.

10. *Westmoreland Republican* quoting *Lancaster Journal,* December 6, 1822, quoted in Kim T. Phillips, "The Pennsylvania Origins of the Jackson Movement," *Political Science Quarterly* 91 (1976): 502.

11. William Plumer, Jr., to William Plumer, January 20, 1825, in Everett Somerville Brown, ed., *The Missouri Compromises and Presidential Politics, 1820–1825* (St. Louis: Missouri Historical Society, 1926), 133.

12. Adams, ed., *Memoirs*, 7:98.
13. Jackson to William B. Lewis, February 14, 1825, to Samuel Swart-
    wout, February 22, 1825, in *PAJ*, 6:29–30, 42.
14. Richardson, 2:882.
15. Houston to Andrew Jackson, January [28], 1827, in *PAJ*, 6:270.
16. Jackson to John Branch, March 3, 1826, in *PAJ*, 6:142–43.
17. Van Buren to Thomas Ritchie, January 13, 1827, Martin Van Buren
    Papers, Library of Congress.

### 3: FIRST-TERM TROUBLES

1. Joseph Story to Mrs. Joseph Story, March 7, 1829, in William W.
   Story, ed., *Life and Letters of Joseph Story* (Boston: C.C. Little and
   J. Brown, 1851), 1:563.
2. Richardson, 2:999–1001.
3. Jackson to John McLemore, April [?], 1829, in *CAJ*, 3:21.
4. *RD*, 22nd Cong., 1st sess., 1325–27.
5. Parton, 3:203–5.
6. Jackson to John Coffee, June 14, 1830, in *CAJ*, 4:146.
7. Jackson to James Hamilton, Jr., June 29, 1828, in *CAJ*, 3:411.
8. The best account is in Robert V. Remini, *Andrew Jackson and the
   Course of American Freedom, 1822–1832* (New York: Harper & Row,
   1981), 233–36.
9. Jackson to James Gadsden, October 12, 1829, in *CAJ*, 4:81; Adams,
   ed., *Memoirs*, 7:89–90; Richardson, 3:1021. On Jackson's policy as
   genocide, see Michael P. Rogin, *Fathers and Children: Andrew Jackson and the Subjugation of the American Indian* (New York: Alfred A.
   Knopf, 1975). For a fair-minded corrective, see Ronald N. Satz,
   "Rhetoric versus Reality: The Indian Policy of Andrew Jackson," in
   William L. Anderson, *Cherokee Removal: Before and After* (Athens:
   University of Georgia Press, 1991), 29–54.
10. Richardson, 2:1053.
11. Ibid., 1000.
12. Kendall to Francis P. Blair, October 2, 1830, Blair-Lee Papers, Prince-
    ton University Library.
13. Jackson to Hugh Lawson White, April 29, 1831, in *CAJ*, 4:272.

### 4: DEMOCRACY AND THE MONSTER BANK

1. Kendall to Blair, March 1, 1830, Blair-Lee Papers, Princeton University Library.
2. Tocqueville, *Democracy in America*, ed. J. P. Mayer (1835–40; Garden City, N.Y.: Doubleday, 1969), 2:389.

3. Jackson to Moses Dawson, July 17, 1830, in *CAJ*, 4:162.

4. J. S. Buckingham, *America, Historical, Statistic, and Descriptive* (London: Fisher, Son & Company, 1841), 2:214.

5. Biddle to Thomas Swann, March 17, 1824, in Senate Documents, 23rd Cong., 2nd sess., no. 17, 297–98.

6. *RD*, 21st Cong., 1st sess., Appendix, 103.

7. Jackson to Hugh Lawson White, April 29, 1831, in *CAJ*, 4:272.

8. Carl B. Swisher, ed., "Roger B. Taney's 'Bank War Manuscript,'" *Maryland Historical Magazine* 53 (1958): 223.

9. Van Buren, *The Autobiography of Martin Van Buren*, ed. John C. Fitzpatrick (1920; New York: Arno Press, 1969), 2:625.

10. Richardson, 2:1139–54.

11. Ibid., 1153.

12. *Morning Courier and Enquirer* (New York), August 24 and 27, 1832.

13. *RD*, 22nd Cong., 1st sess., 1240, 1267; Biddle to Henry Clay, August 1, 1832, in John F. Hopkins et al., *The Papers of Henry Clay* (Lexington: University of Kentucky Press, 1959–92), 8:556.

14. Clay quoted in Merrill D. Peterson, *The Great Triumvirate: Webster, Clay, and Calhoun* (New York: Oxford University Press, 1987), 208.

15. *Boston Daily Advertiser and Patriot*, October 10, 1832, quoted in Robert V. Remini, *Andrew Jackson and the Bank War: A Study in the Growth of Presidential Power* (New York: W.W. Norton, 1967), 101.

16. *Globe*, October 13, 1832; Arthur M. Schlesinger, Jr., and Fred L. Israel, eds., *History of American Presidential Elections, 1789–1968* (New York: Chelsea House, 1985), 2:509; Van Buren to Andrew Donelson, August 26, 1832, Martin Van Buren Papers, Library of Congress; Thurlow Weed, *Autobiography of Thurlow Weed* (Boston: Houghton, Mifflin, 1883), 371–73.

17. *Vermont Patriot*, August 22, 1832, quoted in Remini, *Bank War*, 100. On campaign coverage of the Bank War, see Richard B. Kielbowicz, "Party Press Cohesiveness: Jacksonian Newspapers, 1832," *Journalism Quarterly* 60 (1983): 518–21.

5: THE NULLIFIERS' UPRISING

1. Jackson to John Coffee, July 17, 1832, in *CAJ*, 4:462.

2. James Hamilton, Jr., quoted in William W. Freehling, *The Road to Disunion: Secessionists at Bay, 1776–1854* (New York: Oxford University Press, 1990), 274; Manisha Sinha, *The Counterrevolution of Slavery: Politics and Ideology in Antebellum South Carolina* (Chapel Hill: University of North Carolina Press, 2000), 36–44, quotation on p. 35.

3. William J. Grayson, *Letters of Curtius* (Charleston, S.C.: A. E. Miller, 1851), 8.

4. Calhoun to Virgil Maxcy, September 11, 1830, in Robert L. Meriwether et al., eds., *Papers of John C. Calhoun* (Columbia: University of South Carolina Press, 1959–2003), 21:229.

5. William W. Freehling, *Prelude to Civil War: The Nullification Crisis in South Carolina, 1816–1836* (New York: Harper & Row, 1966), 223; Calhoun to Nathan Towson, September 11, 1830, in Meriwether et al., eds., *Papers of John C. Calhoun*, 21:230–31.

6. Richardson, 2:1162.

7. Clay to Francis Brooke, December 12, 1832, in Hopkins et al., eds., *Papers of Henry Clay*, 8:603.

8. According to one eyewitness, Jackson labored so furiously on the proclamation, writing out memoranda and possible passages with a steel pen, that when he had completed ten pages, the ink on the first was still wet. See Parton, *Jackson*, 3:465–67.

9. Richardson, 2:1203–19.

10. Ibid., 1206, 1211.

11. Paul H. Bergeron, "A Tennessean Blasts Calhoun and Nullification," *Tennessee Historical Quarterly* 26 (1967): 383–86.

12. Jackson to Andrew Crawford, May 1, 1833, in *CAJ*, 5:72; quotation in Richard E. Ellis, *The Union at Risk: Jacksonian Democracy, States' Rights, and the Nullification Crisis* (New York: Oxford University Press, 1987), 159; Petrigu quoted in Sinha, *Counterrevolution*, 60.

13. *The Globe* (Washington, D.C.), August 4, 1832.

14. Marc Friedlander and L. H. Butterfield, eds., *Diary of Charles Francis Adams* (Cambridge, Mass.: Harvard University Press, 1964– ), 5:106.

## 6: THE SECOND BATTLE OF THE BANK

1. Jackson to James K. Polk, December 16, 1832, in *CAJ*, 4:501.

2. Hamilton, *Reminiscences of James A. Hamilton* (New York: Charles Scribner & Company, 1869), 253; Jackson to Martin Van Buren, September 8, 1833, in *CAJ*, 5:183.

3. Kendall to Andrew Jackson, March 20, 1833; Jackson, "Draft of Cabinet Paper, September 18, 1833," in *CAJ*, 5:41–44, 192–203.

4. Biddle to J. G. Watmough, February 8, 1834, in Reginald C. McGrane, ed., *The Correspondence of Nicholas Biddle Dealing with National Affairs, 1807–1844* (Boston: Houghton Mifflin, 1919), 221.

5. James Van Alen to Martin Van Buren, January 27, 1834, Martin Van Buren Papers, Library of Congress; Tuckerman, ed., *Diary of Philip Hone*, 1:184; Samuel Bell to Joseph Blount, February 27, 1834, quoted in Remini, *Bank War*, 131.

6. Parton, *Jackson*, 3:458–50; Everett quoted in Arthur M. Schlesinger, Jr., *The Age of Jackson* (Boston: Little, Brown, 1945), 110–11.
7. *RD*, 23rd Cong., 1st sess., 58–94 (quotation on p. 58).
8. Richardson, 2:1311–12.
9. Quotation in Mary P. Ryan, *Civic Wars: Democracy and Public Life in the American City of the Nineteenth Century* (Berkeley: University of California Press, 1997), 112.
10. *Raleigh Register* (North Carolina), June 10, 1834, in Michael F. Holt, *The Rise and Fall of the American Whig Party: Jacksonian Politics and the Onset of the Civil War* (New York: Oxford University Press, 1999), 29.
11. Seward to Thurlow Weed, April 12, 1835, in Seward, *Autobiography*, 1:258.
12. *Evening Post* (New York), February 4, 1835.
13. *Globe*, January 13, 1835.
14. Ibid., March 29, 1834.
15. *RD*, 23rd Cong., 1st sess., 1092–93; *New York American* quoted in *Cincinnati Daily Gazette*, January 17, 1837.
16. Woodbury quoted in Harry N. Scheiber, "The Pet Banks in Jacksonian Politics and Finance, 1833–1841," *Journal of Economic History* 23 (1963): 208.
17. *RD*, 24th Cong., 2nd sess., 610.
18. Weed to William Henry Seward, April 13, 1835, William Henry Seward Papers, University of Rochester.

7: SLAVERY AND DEMOCRACY

1. Jackson to John Clark, November 23, 1819, in *CAJ*, 2:442; *Genius of Universal Emancipation* (Baltimore), November 8, 1828.
2. John Ashworth, *Slavery, Capitalism, and Politics in the Antebellum Republic*, vol. 1, *Commerce and Compromise* (Cambridge: Cambridge University Press, 1995), 337; *CG*, 25th Cong., 3rd sess., Appendix, 167–75 (quotation on p. 168). On the emergence of the antislavery Jacksonians, see Jonathan H. Earle, *Jacksonian Antislavery and the Politics of Free Soil, 1824–1854* (Chapel Hill: University of North Carolina Press, 2004).
3. Jefferson to Henry Dearborn, August 17, 1821; to W. T. Barry, July 2, 1822, Thomas Jefferson Papers, Library of Congress.
4. Jefferson to John Holmes, April 22, 1820, Thomas Jefferson Papers, Library of Congress; Adams, ed., *Memoirs*, 4:529.
5. Jackson to Andrew J. Donelson, [April 16, 1820], in *PAJ*, 4:367.
6. Eaton to Andrew Jackson, March 11, 1820, in *PAJ*, 4:362; Calhoun to Jackson, June 1, 1820, in *CAJ*, 3:24.

7. Van Buren to Thomas Ritchie, January 13, 1827, Martin Van Buren Papers, Library of Congress.

8. Jackson to Francis Blair, August 22, 1836, Andrew Jackson Papers, Library of Congress.

9. *Globe*, August 22, 29, 1835; Jackson to Amos Kendall, August 9, 1835, in *CAJ*, 5:360.

10. Richardson, 2:1395.

11. On Forsyth and the mails controversy, see Richard R. John, *Spreading the News: The American Postal Service from Franklin to Morse* (Cambridge, Mass.: Harvard University Press, 1995), 278–79.

12. Adams, ed., *Memoirs*, 9:254.

13. *Evening Post*, August 22, 1835; *Emancipator* (New York), November 14, 1836.

14. Van Buren quoted in Donald B. Cole, *Martin Van Buren and the American Political System* (Princeton, N.J.: Princeton University Press, 1984), 261.

15. Van Buren to Nathaniel Macon, February 12, 1836, quoted in ibid., 272.

16. Jackson to Martin Van Buren, January 23, 1838; to Francis Blair, July 19, 1838, in *CAJ*, 5:529, 557.

17. Robinson, *Address to the Voters of the Fifth Congressional District* (n.p., n.d. [1862]), 11; Blair, *A Voice from the Grave of Jackson! Letter from Francis Blair to a Public Meeting in New York, held April 29, 1856* (n.p. [Washington, D.C.: Buell & Blanchard], 1856), 3.

## 8: PUSHING WESTWARD

1. *Cherokee Nation v. State of Georgia*, 5 Peters 1 (1831).

2. *Worcester v. Georgia*, 31 U.S. 515 (1832).

3. [Lundy], *War in Texas: A Review of the Facts and Circumstances* (1836; Philadelphia: Merrihew & Gunn, 1837), 3.

4. Richardson, 2:1469.

## 9: JACKSON'S LEGACY

1. Thomas Hart Benton, *Thirty Years' View; or, A History of the Working of the American Government for Thirty Years, from 1820 to 1850* (New York: D. Appleton, 1854–56), 1:735.

2. Richardson, 2:1518, 1524.

3. Richardson, 2:1513–14, 1525.

4. Jackson to Andrew J. Donelson, March 12, 1835, quoted in Robert V. Remini, *Andrew Jackson and the Course of American Democracy, 1832–1845* (New York: Harper & Row, 1984), 339.

5. Richardson, 2:1524; *Globe,* July 1, 1839.

6. George Bancroft, quoting Jackson, in Remini, *Jackson and the Course of American Democracy,* 343.

7. *RD,* 23rd Cong., 1st sess., 1375.

8. Richardson, 1:310; Jefferson to Levi Lincoln, October 25, 1802, Thomas Jefferson Papers, Library of Congress.

9. Van Buren, *Autobiography,* 1:303.

10. Jackson to Andrew J. Donelson, July 9, 1840, quoted in Remini, *Jackson and the Course of American Democracy,* 465; Jackson to Martin Van Buren, July 31, 1840, in *CAJ,* 6:68.

11. Jackson to Francis Blair, April 19, 1841, in *CAJ,* 6:105.

12. Jackson to Francis Blair, May 11, 1844, in ibid., 286.

13. Polk to Cave Johnson, December 21, 1844, in "Letters of James K. Polk to Cave Johnson, 1833–1844," *Tennessee Historical Magazine* 1 (1915): 254.

14. Quotation in Remini, *Jackson and the Course of American Democracy,* 524.

15. CG, 25th Cong., 3rd sess., Appendix, 167–75 (quotation on p. 168).

16. *Signal of Liberty* (Ann Arbor, Mich.), September 15, October 12, 1841.

17. Jackson to Jesse Duncan Elliott, March 27, 1845, in *CAJ,* 6:391.

# Milestones

1767 Born March 15 in Waxhaw settlement on the border of North and South Carolina.

1775–80 Attends schools run by Dr. William Humphries and James White Stephenson.

1780–81 Serves as boy soldier in the American Revolution, captured and maimed by the British, and later released in a prisoner exchange. Death of his mother, Elizabeth, leaves him bereft of his entire immediate family.

1782–86 Attends and then teaches school; moves to Salisbury, North Carolina, and studies law.

1787 Licensed as an attorney.

1788 Appointed public prosecutor for western North Carolina (later Tennessee) and settles in Nashville.

1791 Marries Rachel Donelson Robards, a ceremony that will have to be repeated three years later due to legal irregularities in her marital status.

1795 Elected delegate to Tennessee Constitutional Convention.

1796 Elected to the U.S. House of Representatives; defeated in election for major general of Tennessee militia.

1797 Elected to the U.S. Senate.

1798 Resigns Senate seat; returns to Nashville; elected judge of Superior Court of Tennessee.

1802 Elected major general of Tennessee militia.

1804 Resigns as judge; buys Hermitage property.

1805–07 Participates in the Burr conspiracy.

1806 Kills Charles Dickinson in a duel.

1809 Adopts Andrew Jackson Donelson, son of Elizabeth and Severn Donaldson.

1812–14 Leads troops against Creek Indians, British, and Spanish.

1815   Defeats British at Battle of New Orleans on January 8.

1816–20   Signs treaties with Cherokees, Chickasaws, and Chocktaws.

1817–18   Assumes command of Seminole War and invades Florida.

1821   Appointed governor of Florida Territory; serves eleven weeks, then resigns and returns to Tennessee.

1822   Nominated for president of the United States by Tennessee legislature.

1823   Elected to U.S. Senate.

1824   Nominated for president by the Pennsylvania legislature; receives a plurality of popular and electoral vote.

1825   Defeated for president in House vote; accuses Henry Clay and John Quincy Adams of a "Corrupt Bargain"; resigns Senate seat and is nominated for president by Tennessee legislature.

1826–28   Campaigns for president, supported by Martin Van Buren and John C. Calhoun.

1828   Elected seventh president of the United States.

1829–31   Involved in Eaton controversy.

1830   Confronts Calhoun on state rights and past political criticism; signs Indian Removal Bill; vetoes Maysville Road Bill.

1831   Reshuffles his cabinet.

1832   Vetoes Bank Bill; wins reelection to second term; makes preparations to resist South Carolina nullification; issues Nullification Proclamation.

1833   Sends Force Bill to Congress and later signs it along with compromise Tariff of 1833; begins removal of deposits from the Second Bank of the United States.

1834   Censured by the U.S. Senate; his reply to censure rejected by the Senate; signs Coinage Act.

1835   Demands Van Buren's nomination as president; responds to crisis over abolitionist mailings in Charleston, South Carolina.

1836   Signs Deposit Bill and issues Specie Circular; recognizes Texas independence.

1837   Issues Farewell Address; attends Van Buren's inauguration, then departs for retirement in Tennessee.

1840   Campaigns for Van Buren in Tennessee.

1844   Endorses James K. Polk for president; persuades President John Tyler to withdraw from the race; supports Texas annexation.

1845   Dies at the Hermitage, June 8, and buried two days later in the Hermitage garden.

# Selected Bibliography

There are two principal printed collections of Jackson's papers, *Correspondence of Andrew Jackson*, edited by John Spencer Bassett (Washington, D.C.: The Carnegie Institution, 1926–35); and the continuing *Papers of Andrew Jackson* (Knoxville: University of Tennessee Press, 1980– ), edited by Sam B. Smith, Harriet Chappell Owsley, and others. At the time this book went to press, the latter was complete through 1828. Jackson's official messages and addresses as president are presented in the second volume of James D. Richardson, ed., *A Compilation of the Messages and Papers of the President* (Washington, D.C.: Bureau of National Literature and Art, 1910). A modern, authoritative selection of Jackson's major writings, including the major addresses from his presidency, is long overdue.

Where doing so did not obscure the author's meaning, I have kept quotations as originally written, or as quoted in various secondary sources. Where unnoted, my presentation of the facts of Jackson's life and presidency (although not necessarily my interpretations) relies on the massive literature on Jackson, the high points of which are listed below. Two biographies of Jackson are essential, however, for any student of the man and his times.

A great deal of valuable primary material as well as provocative analysis appears in Robert V. Remini's exhaustive study, published in three volumes: *Andrew Jackson and the Course of American Empire, 1767–1821; Andrew Jackson and the Course of American Freedom,*

*1822–1832;* and *Andrew Jackson and the Course of American Democracy, 1833–1845* (New York: Harper & Row, 1977, 1981, 1984). A one-volume abridgment of Remini's massive work appeared in paperback in 1988. Remini is unquestionably the premier student in our time of Jackson, but there is still a good deal to be learned from and enjoyed in James Parton's classic three-volume *Life of Andrew Jackson* (New York: Mason Brothers, 1860). A new one-volume biography, by H. W. Brands, appeared while the present book was in press.

I wrote *Andrew Jackson* just after completing a much longer work, *The Rise of American Democracy: Jefferson to Lincoln* (New York: W. W. Norton, 2005). Some of the themes, formulations, and interpretations advanced in this brief biography receive more extended treatment there. I am extremely grateful, though, to have had the opportunity to take another look at Jackson, which alerted me to some important nuances about his life and his presidency that earlier I either slighted or entirely missed.

This selected bibliography from the enormous literature on Jackson and Jacksonian politics includes the chief biographies (apart from Remini's and Parton's), as well as books and articles that are particularly informative about aspects of Jackson's presidency. It also lists works I believe are indicative of the shifting interpretive trends since 1945 about the Jacksonian era.

Ashworth, John. *Slavery, Capitalism, and Politics in the Antebellum Republic.* Vol. 1, *Commerce and Compromise.* Cambridge: Cambridge University Press, 1995.

Bassett, John Spencer. *The Life of Andrew Jackson.* Garden City, N.Y.: Doubleday, Page, 1911.

Belohlavek, John M. *"Let the Eagle Soar": The Foreign Policy of Andrew Jackson.* Lincoln: University of Nebraska Press, 1985.

Benson, Lee. *The Concept of Jacksonian Democracy: New York as a Test Case.* Princeton, N.J.: Princeton University Press, 1961.

Burstein, Andrew. *The Passions of Andrew Jackson.* New York: Alfred A. Knopf, 2003.

Cole, Donald B. *The Presidency of Andrew Jackson.* Lawrence: University of Kansas Press, 1993.

————. *Martin Van Buren and the American Political System*. Princeton, N.J.: Princeton University Press, 1984.

Cooper Jr., William J. *The South and the Politics of Slavery, 1828–1856*. Baton Rouge: Louisiana State University Press, 1978.

Curtis, James C. *Andrew Jackson and the Search for Vindication*. Boston: Little, Brown, 1976.

Earle, Jonathan H. *Jacksonian Antislavery and the Politics of Free Soil, 1824–1854*. Chapel Hill: University of North Carolina Press, 2004.

Ellis, Richard E. *The Union at Risk: Jacksonian Democracy, States' Rights, and the Nullification Crisis*. New York: Oxford University Press, 1987.

Feller, Daniel. *The Jacksonian Promise: America, 1815–1840*. Baltimore: Johns Hopkins University Press, 1995.

Freehling, William W. *The Road to Disunion: Secessionists at Bay, 1776–1854*. New York: Oxford University Press, 1990.

Hammond, Bray. *Banks and Politics in America from the Revolution to the Civil War*. Princeton, N.J.: Princeton University Press, 1957.

Hofstadter, Richard. *The American Political Tradition and the Men Who Made It*. New York: Alfred A. Knopf, 1948.

————. *The Idea of a Party System: The Rise of Legitimate Opposition in the United States, 1780–1840*. Berkeley: University of California Press, 1969.

Holt, Michael F. *The Rise and Fall of the American Whig Party: Jacksonian Politics and the Onset of the Civil War*. New York: Oxford University Press, 1999.

James, Marquis. *Andrew Jackson: The Border Captain*. Indianapolis: Bobbs Merrill, 1933.

————. *Andrew Jackson: Portrait of a President*. Indianapolis: Bobbs Merrill, 1937.

Kohl, Lawrence Frederick. *The Politics of Individualism: Parties and the American Character in the Jacksonian Era*. New York: Oxford University Press, 1989.

Latner, Richard B. *The Presidency of Andrew Jackson: White House Politics, 1829–1837*. Athens: University of Georgia Press, 1979.

McCormick, Richard P. *The Second Party American System: Party Formation in the Jacksonian Era*. Chapel Hill: University of North Carolina Press, 1966.

McFaul, John M. *The Politics of Jacksonian Finance*. Ithaca, N.Y.: Cornell University Press, 1972.

————. "Expediency vs. Morality: Slavery and Jacksonian Politics." *Journal of American History* 62 (June 1975): 24–39.

Meyers, Marvin. *The Jacksonian Persuasion: Politics and Belief*. Stanford, Calif.: Stanford University Press, 1957.

Rogin, Michael Paul. *Fathers and Children: Andrew Jackson and the Subjugation of the American Indian*. New York: Alfred A. Knopf, 1975.

Satz, Ronald N. *American Indian Policy in the Jacksonian Era*. Lincoln: University of Nebraska Press, 1975.

Schlesinger, Jr., Arthur M. *The Age of Jackson*. Boston: Little, Brown, 1945.

Sellers, Charles. *The Market Revolution: Jacksonian America, 1815–1846*. New York: Oxford University Press, 1991.

Ward, John William. *Andrew Jackson—Symbol for an Age*. New York: Oxford University Press, 1955.

Watson, Harry L. *Liberty and Power: The Politics of Jacksonian America*. New York: Hill & Wang, 1990.

Wilson, Major L. *Space, Time, and Freedom: The Quest for Nationality and the Irrepressible Conflict*. Westport, Conn.: Greenwood Press, 1974.

Wood, Kirsten. "'One Woman So Dangerous to Public Morals': Gender and Power in the Eaton Affair." *Journal of the Early Republic* 17 (Summer 1997): 237–75.

Young, Mary B. *Redskins, Ruffleshirts, and Rednecks: Indian Allotments in Alabama and Mississippi, 1830–1860*. Norman: University of Oklahoma Press, 1961.

# Acknowledgments

Being asked by my friend Arthur Schlesinger, Jr., to write a book on Andrew Jackson was a special honor, for which I am deeply grateful. I can only hope the results approach the standard he set sixty years ago for all historians of the Jackson era.

Robert V. Remini and Ted Widmer, authors of the volumes in this series on Jackson's predecessor and successor, lent their encouragement and expertise. I am especially indebted to Bob Remini for catching some errors and infelicities that otherwise would have snuck through.

Paul Golob of Times Books/Henry Holt has been a generous and patient overseer of this entire project. Thanks to him, I had the great good fortune to work closely with Robin Dennis, also of Times Books, who edited the manuscript with exceptional care and intelligence.

# Index

# ABOUT THE AUTHOR

———

Sean Wilentz, the Dayton-Stockon Professor of History and the director of the Program in American Studies at Princeton University, is the author or editor of eight previous books, including *Chants Democratic* and *The Rise of American Democracy*. He has also written on contemporary politics and history for *The New York Times*, the *Los Angeles Times*, *The New Republic*, and other publications. He lives in Princeton, New Jersey.